☞ All Rights Reserved. ☜

BOTHWELL:
An Historical Drama.

For Private Circulation.

James Hepburn,
Fourth Earl of Bothwell,
Third Husband of Mary Stuart, Queen of Scotland.

BOTHWELL: 1536-78

(JAMES HEPBURN, FOURTH EARL OF BOTHWELL, THIRD HUSBAND
OF MARY, QUEEN OF SCOTS.)

An Historical Drama.

Bothwell's Book Mark.

BY

 JOHN WATTS DE PEYSTER.

New York:
CHARLES H. LUDWIG, PRINTER, 10 & 12 READE STREET.
1884.

TO THE

DAIMON,

(Δαιμων, Genius),

OF

PYTHAGORAS,

(VI. Century B. C.)

WHO FIRST TAUGHT TO THE WESTERN WORLD THE

BUDDHISTIC DOCTRINE

OF THE

TRANSMIGRATION OF SOULS

THROUGH DIFFERENT SUCCESSIVE HUMAN BODIES; AND TO THAT

SPIRIT

WHICH ANIMATED

SEMIRAMIS, CLEOPATRA AND MARY STUART,

AND NOW MANIFESTS ITSELF IN

THIS DRAMA IS DEDICATED.

COPYRIGHT, 1884, BY J. WATTS DE PEYSTER.

BOTHWELL:

AN HISTORICAL DRAMA.

INTRODUCTION.

"It is difficult to estimate facts delivered under circumstances which deprive the testimony of all moral value ; when falsehood is not an accident, but a property of the speaker's character, and is not the error of a moment or the crime of an individual; but an organic system." "*Nimrod*," II., 494 ; HIGGIN'S "*Anacalypsis*," II., 42.

Quite a library of works had been already collected and consulted and compared with others almost as numerous in public libraries, before the writer gave to the world the first of his Trilogy, entitled "Mary Queen of Scots: A Study." After that was published, he found that the subject had enlisted the pens of able men all over Europe, whose works were unknown in this country and some of them even in England and Scotland, except to a very small number whose studies led in this particular direction. Orders were immediately sent out to different book-centres and a number of rare as well as recent treatises rewarded the search.

The second of the Trilogy, "James Hepburn, Earl of Bothwell: A Vindication," was a work of much less labor than the first. Shortly after this appeared, still farther research revealed new authorities ; and after an examination, analysis and comparison, even more elaborate than the two previous ones, appeared the Third of the Trilogy : "An Inquiry into the Career and Character of Mary Stuart ("*Crux Criticorum*"), ("The puzzle of critics"), and a Justification of Bothwell. ("*Audire est operæ Pretium*.") ("What is herein disclosed is worthy of attention.") Scarcely had this been published when a number of catalogues, containing the names of still further authorities, which had escaped previous inquests, were transmitted from various friends, collectors, librarians and students ; and, as the result of all this, the writer's private library on Mary Stuart, which at first required only one large case, would now fill several.

At Edinburgh, Scotland, 1883, was published a very interesting work, by the Reverend Joseph Stevenson, S. J. (Jesuit), entitled "The History of Mary Stuart, from the Murder of Rizzio until her Flight into England. By Claude Nau, her secretary. Now first printed from the original manuscripts, with illustrative papers from the secret archives of the Vatican and other collections in Rome."

Doubtless, besides this manuscript of Nau, others of equal importance, perhaps, lie hidden among the uncollated documents of some of the public libraries in Rome, Spain, Paris, England and Scotland, or among the family archives of prominent Scottish families, whose ancestors were connected with events transpiring during the reign of Mary Stuart. Such documents may also exist in the collections left by the descendants of the envoys or agents sent over by the French Government to the Court of Mary. Careful search might even discover something contemporary among the papers left behind by the different representatives of England, in Scotland, between the dates of the birth of Mary and the accession of James, her son, to the crowns of Scotland and England. There should be documents of the highest importance relating to Bothwell in the appropriate public depositories at Copenhagen or some of the Royal Residences—although so many of the latter have been destroyed by fire that it would be very easy to account for the absence of such authorities. Nor should the possibility of solving problems of the greatest interest, now involved in mystery, in regard to the last years of Bothwell, be abandoned until the last scrap of parchment or paper preserved by the families of the nobility of Scania, has been scrutinized with extreme care. Something might even be found at Stockholm or Upsala, whither so many old collections gradually found their way; or at Skokloster, that castle-mine or bonanza of the secrets and curiosities of the past, since the fingers of the Wrangels seem to have been like those of Jack Sheppard, perfect "lime twigs," to which everything remarkable that came in contact with them was almost sure to adhere.

The names of the works obtained, as well as of those examined (if the latter are not too numerous), will be appended to complete the "List of Authorities." published at pages 209, 210, 211, of Number Three of the Trilogy previously referred to.

The fact is, that the investigation of the careers and characters of Mary Stuart and of Bothwell, which at first was an amusement or an occupation, has become almost a passion ; because the deeper that the writer has plunged into historical research, the more convincing has become the proof that in these, as in very many other cases, political, personal and religious prejudices and partialities, falsehood, not truth, have painted the portraits of the unfortunate Queen, and the still more unfortunate Bothwell, her third husband—the latter the most unhappy in life as well as in death,—seeing that Mary has found a multitude of defenders ; whereas those who champion her cause vie with her worst enemies in striving to blacken the character of Bothwell ; seeming to be convinced within themselves that one among the surest methods to rehabilitate her character is to demonstrate that she was the victim of a villain, Bothwell ; whereas he, in fact, was victim of her, as well as of her bastard brother, the Earl of Murray, finally Regent of Scotland— than whom a falser man and in many respects a greater political villain never lived ; except in so far that, in a period of barbarism and sensuality, he found sufficient employment in accomplishing the ruin of Mary, Bothwell, Darnley, in fact whoever stood in his way ; to let the the three German W's, "*Wein, Weibern und Wurfel*,"—Wine or wassail, women and gambling ;—especially women, as paramours, of whom to his sorrow his father, James V., was so fond, severely alone.

Among the many curious books on this subject obtained from Germany, is one entitled "*Maria, Königin von Schottland*, von Friedrich Gentz. Braunschweig, 1799."

It is a diminutive quarto and presents, together with a certainly unique portrait, two other engravings, one of the Murder of Rizzio, and the other of Mary taking leave of her servants before execution ;—but the most curious feature of it is, that few of the pages are of equal size—some are quarto shape, some duodecimo, and some even more irregular in shape.

Another even more curious work, entitled "*La Covr Sainte Dv. R. Pere Nicolas Cavssin de la compagnie de Iesvs*. Mise en vn Bel

Ordre. Avec vne notable augmentation des Vies des personnes illustres de la Cour, taut du vieil que du nouveau Testament. Et augmentée en cette derniere Edition de la vie de l'Autheur et de diuerses Histoires. [Two volumes in one. Folio, large.] A Paris, chez Iean. Dv. Bray, rue Sainte Iaques, aux Espics meurs et au Chapelier (?) M.DC.LIII. avec privilege, et approbation."

The likeness of Mary Stuart, Queen of Scots, attached to this book very much resembles a number in the possession of the writer (who has collected perhaps a hundred different engravings, &c.), and presents an additional proof that Mary's fascination lay more in her "marvelous agreableness," her grace, accomplishments, language, manner and expression, than in the mere physical beauties of form, face and features, by which the vast majorities of the male sex are completely carried away.

Without putting much faith in the statements of a member of the Society of Jesus — a Jesuit; nevertheless, on the principle, that the devil may quote Scripture appositely — Father Caussin is not far out of the way in his estimate of the Earl of Murray. He says (II. 308), "that he was a dangerous and dissolute man." If by "dissolute" he means a man whose ambition knew no restraint of morals, he is perfectly correct, and especially when he adds that Murray was a mere instrument in the hands of Queen Elizabeth, and scattered the seeds that germinated and produced a harvest of tragedies. After having filled his lungs with breath of a furious and turbulent ambition, which was breathed into them by Knox, the patriarch of the Scottish Reformers, Murray never ceased to assume the quality of Regent and aspire to the authority of King without sparing any detestable wickedness by which he could arrive at the goal of his desires. To avert Mary's marriage with a foreign prince, which might have buttressed her own with a sufficient power to assert her authority, he managed to throw her into the arms of Darnley, hoping thereby to insure the real administration to himself. Finding that, in consequence of Mary's passion for her boy-husband, he, Murray, was likely to fail of his object, he determined to get rid of the latter. Murray possessed at the Court of Scotland an agent in the Earl of Morton, who was nothing more than his *Alter Ego*. To him he confided the commission of throwing the apple of discord into the marriage-bed of the King and Queen. This Morton accomplished with incredible artifice, so that this master-mechanic of iniquity was able to kindle two furnaces with the same breath, unceasingly firing the heart of the Queen with proofs of her husband's miserable conduct, and at the same time lighting in the bosom of the latter ambitious aspirations which were the more hateful in that they were the offspring of an ingratitude which was based at once on a detestable character and cowardice.

In all this the Jesuit ignores the latent influence of Mary's long-seated prediliction for the Earl of Bothwell, which like the etherial circulation of the impalpable force-imparting fluid through the tubes of the nerves, is just as necessary to the vitality of man as the perceptible ebb and flow of the visible red blood, which is life itself. Murray's influence through various agencies, of whom Morton was the chief, brought about the murder of Rizzio—a blow which was aimed as much at Mary and the child in her womb, afterwards James VI., as at the miserable musician, minister of state and papal emissary, who was stabbed and almost slain at the very feet of the Queen.

The miserable prince whom jealousy had impelled to the murder of the favorite, was now the next obstacle which stood in Murray's path. Mary's love for Bothwell and his life-long love for her, were to be converted into elements of destruction for both. Murray and his co-conspirators felt that if Bothwell and the Queen could be implicated in the murder of Darnley, and then be mutually guilty of adultery and assassination, and finally united in marriage, public opinion could be so excited against them that Bothwell would be driven from the kingdom and ruined irremediably, Mary thrust from her throne, blasted in character, and the whole authority and its advantages remain at the disposal of Murray and his co-partners in iniquity. The story of what followed reads as if the successive results were simply a rehearsal of the details of the plan.

The good Jesuit tells the story, in some respects, sufficiently well that it will be interesting simply to translate some of the passages of his almost obsolete French. "Some time after the death of the king [Darnley], Bothwell, who was one of the powerful noblemen in Scotland, dared to seek the Queen in marriage, since the Earl of Murray had promised that, as a recompense of his crime." [Putting Darnley out of the way.]   *   *   *

In order to reconcile Mary to the match with a man who " was suspected of so detestable a deed—even if he was innocent, besides being already married; the bastard, Murray, and the other conspirators who had undertaken this affair with such obstinate resolution, managed to have the criminal acquitted by judges who belonged to their faction; and furthermore arranged matters, so as to satisfy the Queen as to the removal of the other obstacle, a living wife."   *   *   *   Father Caussin then proceeds to describe how this Philistine [Bothwell] adored this lovely arch of alliance, the willing captive of his bow and spear at Almond Bridge.

" It was on this occasion that the Earl of Murray, who had withdrawn a little, so as to avoid any suspicion of being concerned in the murder of Darnley, returned to court and encouraged the suit of the King's murderer, rewarding him with the conquest of the most beautiful Queen in the world, in full payment of what he had done. Murray did not cease to press Mary to accept Bothwell as her husband, urging upon her the public avowal of the Earl's innocence, the splendor of his house, his courageous exploits and the proofs of his fidelity, all of which rendered him worthy of her love. He added that being alone, and without support, she was utterly incapable of settling the difficulties which had been excited against her, to meet the plots which could be formed against her authority, and to sustain the weighty charge of the kingdom; moreover, that she would accept as her husband, and for the companion of her fortune and her designs, one [Bothwell] who had the power, the will and the courage to oppose her, if she did not do so; and that she would never have peace with him, except by the consummation of such a wise arrangement. By these counsels this miserable man promised himself, either to reign through his confidant [Bothwell] or to degrade the Queen, by her own act, and thus deprive her of her authority; all which he did. The marriage was accomplished, and the pressing solicitations of the Earl of Bothwell finally won the heart of Mary, who espoused him in the face of the Church with all the requisite ceremonies. Some writers have recorded that this gentle soul was greatly persecuted by these proposals of marriage on account of her beauty and that the facility of her natural disposition, which had not sufficient powers of resistance against the pressing importunity and the continual battle, which love arrayed against her, brought upon her a fearful deluge of misfortunes."

Finally, to close these citations, the same author states that Mary, even in bidding Bothwell to leave her at Carberry Hill, acknowledged that his courage and his worth were sufficient to guarantee her against his storm which was ready to burst upon her head. Alas! she did not possess the moral courage to act up to the convictions of her reason. These citations have not been made with any other view than to demonstrate that the Jesuit author, in his biography, justifies the writer in his bad opinion of Murray, as well as in his high estimate of Bothwell, as one of the most powerful of the Scottish nobility, renowned for the greatest exploits, of an admitted capacity sufficient to rule the kingdom, desperately in love with Mary and culpable only, or rather weak, in suffering himself to be made the instrument of Murray and the latter's co-conspirators simply to aid him to win the woman that he loved and to enable them to accomplish their designs. Had he been as base and crafty as Murray, he might by a similar course of fraud, injustice and embezzlement have built up a party; but being, in spite of all his faults, a fearless honest man, he fell, because being alone and without a political party he could not maintain himself against an organized party—like that which has ruled and robbed this city of New York for so many years, backed by a fanaticized multitude, greedy for spoil and offices.

In the following historical drama there is not an incident or remark for which one or more authorities cannot be produced, except at the close of the Second Act, when Bothwell is represented as coming on to the rescue of the Queen. It is a slight anachronism. He did attempt to rescue her at the moment, and he did so afterward, and enabled her to re-establish her authority; but it was not until a few days had elapsed. Again, the language placed in the mouths of the speakers is not, word for word, the same that they wrote or spoke; but the ideas are identically the same, and very often the utterances are textually correct, with the exception that the broad Scotch or rude English of the sixteenth century and the French is presented in the words and forms of the present day. In all other respects, this is an attempt to arrange the momentous occurrences of the most important phases of the reign of Queen Mary in a succession of Acts, Scenes and Tableaux, so that they may be placed upon the stage with ample opportunity for a display of acting and setting such as are rarely afforded by a drama that realizes the exact truths of history and biography, without distorting or exaggerating either of them; literally presenting, to use the words of a quaint poet—

> "The loves and troubles of Queen Mary,
> Revealed for him that reads,
> And whether she was over chary
> In all her acts and deeds."

CHARACTERS.

DARNLEY, King-Consort, Second Husband of Mary, Queen of Scotland.
JAMES HEPBURN, FOURTH EARL OF BOTHWELL, afterwards third Husband of the Queen, died in the Danish State-prison, Dragsholm.

James Hepburn, Fourth Earl of Bothwell; Duke of Orkney, &c., &c.; Third Husband of Mary Stuart, Queen of Scotland;
as he appeared in Tournament and on the Battlefield.

THE EARL OF MURRAY, illegitimate Half-Brother of the Queen, afterward Regent of Scotland, murdered.
JAMES DOUGLAS, FOURTH EARL OF MORTON, subsequently Regent of Scotland. Beheaded under James VI., son of Mary and Darnley.
GEORGE, EARL OF HUNTLEY, brother-in-law of Bothwell.
LORD ROBERT STUART, Commendator of Holyrood Abbey, illegitimate brother of the Queen.

LORD RUTHVEN, died of consequences of fever—the relapse on his leaving his sick bed to assist in the murder of Rizzio. James VI., Son of Mary and Darnley, rooted out the family.

LORD LINDESAY, one of the most truculent of the Scottish aristocracy.

ALEXANDER, FIFTH LORD HOME, died in the dungeon to which Morton consigned him.

SIR ARCHIBALD DOUGLAS, "that priest-bred manager of plots," cousin and agent of Morton.

SIR JAMES BALFOUR "'the most corrupt man of a most evil age,'" betrayed by his wife, Morton's mistress, thrown into a dungeon in Morton's castle of Dalkeith.

SIR WILLIAM MAITLAND OF LETHINGTON, the Chameleon, one of the ablest and most unprincipled statesmen of his century. Poisoned himself to escape the disgrace of an infamous public execution.

SIR WILLIAM KIRKALDY OF GRANGE, an admirable soldier and experienced military leader, but a weak man, a most untrustworthy subject, and a spy, and paid agent of the English ministry. Hanged like a dog by Morton.

} now enemies of the Queen, afterwards her last supporters in arms in Scotland.

SIR ANDREW KERR, of Faudonside, whose brutality at the murder of Rizzio, MARY would never pardon.

SIR GEORGE DOUGLAS, Postulate of Aberborthwick, natural son of the Earl of Angus.

SIR JAMES MELVIL, Page, then Courtier, Adviser and Friend of Queen Mary.

PATRICK BELLENDEN, a Conspirator.

THE PREBENDARY, ROBERT BALFOUR.

DAVID RIZZIO, originally an Italian Musician, Confidential Foreign Secretary or Minister of the Queen.

BETON, LAIRD OF CREICH, one of the Queen's Masters of her Household.

ARTHUR ERSKINE, the Queen's Equerry.

ANTHONY STANDEN, a gallant young English refugee, the Queen's Page.

NICHOLAS HUBERT, known as "French Paris."
HAY, LAIRD OF TALLA.
JOHN HEPBURN, of Bolton.
THE "BLACK" ORMISTON.
CAPTAIN BLACKADDER.

} Retainers of Bothwell, executed under the Regent Murray.

WILLIAM TAYLOR, Darnley's Page or Body-servant.

MARY STUART, QUEEN OF SCOTS.

JANE, COUNTESS OF ARGYLE, illegitimate sister of the Queen.

MARY BEATOUN, faithful life-long favorite and attendant of the Queen, one of the "Four Maries:" niece of Cardinal Beatoun, assassinated by Kirkaldy of Grange and others.
LADY RERES, Chamber Lady to the Queen and Confidant of Bothwell.
Attendants on the Queen and Nobles, People attached to the Queen's Household, Royal Hackbutters (Musketeers), Constables for the Service of the Artillery (Artillerists), Troopers, Pikemen, &c., &c.

Bothwell—with Hagbutteers (Musketeers), Archers and Border Pikemen.

In an historical drama which inevitably requires the concurrence of so many characters, the number of actors brought upon the stage must conform to the probable strength of a company at the disposal of a single manager. Therefore, it may be necessary to reduce the number of parts, and consolidate the action and language of several persons into one representative on the stage. Thus, while the incidents of the drama are strictly true, all the characters who played their parts on the real stage of life need not appear upon the mimic boards of the theatre.

James Hepburn,
Fourth Earl of Bothwell.

AN HISTORICAL DRAMA.

ACT I.

SCENE I.—*A bosket or bower of evergreens, clipped yew, in the garden of Holyrood Palace.* MARY BEATOUN *and* LADY RERES *come forward as the curtain rises.*

Holyrood Palace.

MARY BEATOUN (*evidently continuing a confidential conversation*).
    You do amaze me, Lady Reres. Yet,
Standing so high in confidence of both—
Our lovely Queen and Scotland's proudest Earl—
You must know much escapes less favor'd mortals.
Does the Queen love the Earl, and as you say,
With fonder, firmer force than she loved Darnley?
Does she love Bothwell so?

LADY RERES.   Indeed she does :
              And she hath found in him a nobler mate
              Than any yet on whom she's fix'd her choice :
              The rest were boys. In him she's found a man :
              A rough one it is true, but still a man :
              A diamond not all polish'd, but a man :
              Hepburn's a jewel meet for Mary Stuart,
              They greet at him, but such as he can scorn
              The calculating, hypocritic guile
              Of foxy Morton ; Knox's fav'rite Murray,
              Who leaves to baser instruments the deed,
              And looks at evil through, between, his fingers ;
              Ready to pluck the fruit when 'tis matur'd
              Upon the muck heap fully fed its growth ;
              And if *for him* cares not how 't grew or grows.
              James Hepburn, with his mail'd and stalwart hand
              Plucks the ripe ear at once with fearless front ;
              He is no coward. 'Mid false, sordid "Bonds"
              That rule this Scotland, he *alone* is true.
              Poor he has been, despite his lofty birth,
              So poor he's lack'd a single golden piece
              To pay his score : yet never took a bribe
              To wrong his country for a foreign quean :—
              He never sold his honor to Queen Bess,
              As other nobles flout at faithfulness
              So that their jerkins gleam at Tudor cost.
              His creed he's clung to spite of ev'ry wile,
              Nor ever made, like Murray, creed the cloak
              To hide intent, and set the kiln on fire
              That burn'd our land, ay, to the very bone,
              So that it prov'd alembic whence t' extract
              Gain, influence, power, for selfish ends.
              Hepburn's no hypocrite ! He loves Mary
              For Mary Stuart's sake, and will not yield
              A single inch to foreign lure or price,
              Content to risk the loss of all he seeks
              Rather than sacrifice the faith is his.
              Sin ! he may sin against his own brave soul,
              But never 'gainst what he deems great and true
              To foster his ambition. The people
              Know well that in his soul there burns the fire
              For Scotland's Independence flaming high.
              The nobles love him not. He scorns their lies,

Their moral weakness and their selfish strength,
However brave in brawl and shedding blood.
Among the nobles, Hepburn's not a friend ;
But 'mid the people, duly weigh'd 's the man :
There's not a lord is held in such content
And honest admiration. This makes Mary,
Despising such a coward thing as Darnley,
Seek to break loose from brilliant toy she once,
With love begotten through the eye, not reason,
So madly wed, and long to link her fate
With one who, once beside her on the throne,
Fit mate would be for queen to mate withal :
And brave as she, throw banner to the winds,
And say to England, Come what storm come may,
I and my husband will confront it boldly !

MARY B. Each word you utter 's like revealing dawn,
Breaking through clouds after a starless night.

LADY R. Many a village maid, in face and form—
The child of Nature 's far more beautiful
Than Mary, Queen, so peerless in men's eyes :—
But she's a queen, therefore a deity,
And, to defects, all, blinded by her rank,
Behold in her, Anadyomene :
She's not so lovely as report declares—
Although most lovable as all admit—
She is too tall, too vig'rous in her port :
A full man's heart is beating in her bosom ;
And more than once she pray'd to be a man
With helm on head and girt with sword and dagg,
Astride a gallant steed like Border Chief :
Yet in her eye there's such demoniac light
Can kindle passion in a breast of ice,
And lure, as serpent fascinates a bird : —
We've seen her do it. Blazing into flame
Her heat could melt a lump of iron ore :
'Tis not her beauty won her Hepburn's love
But something kin to tropic heat at pole.
Magnificently clad, her lusty form
Captures the men as springtime 'livens flies :
And though she plays, as cat plays with a mouse,
With lovers bowing 'fore her sov'reign grace,
By never yielding has Earl Bothwell won :
As spell more potent overcomes the less :

And binds the weaker with more potent sway :
His magic's been an over-mast'ring will.
Her father's grandeur and her Guise finesse
Make her omnipotent in swaying men.
When young she rul'd them with her gentle lures.
A full grown woman with her subtle wiles :
And thus, pre-eminent in female guile,
She leads the wolves as Orpheus moved the trees : —
Carried away by Darnley's courtly airs,
She soon discerned the caitiff 'neath the style,
And then returning to a stifled love.
She found herself compell'd, as 't were by Fate,
To the embrace of stalwart Bothwell's arms,
As hunted deer rush wildly in the net.

MARY B. You astonish me! I'll keep *this* secret,
And, silent, watch th' unfolding of events :
The Queen has grown to brook no contradiction,
And visits with disfavor all who cross her—
Moreover, I remember Chastellar,
And handsome John of Gordon. I will not
Have gallant Hepburn's blood upon my conscience.
Mary is Queen. 'Tis she is highest judge
Come let us in ! (*Church bell rings.*) I hear the Compline bell,
And as the Mass grows less in favor, we
Of the true faith must be the more attent
Upon our duties, and so please the Queen.
(*They go out conversing.*)

SCENE II.—*A Rere-supper in an apartment of the lodgings of the* EARL OF MORTON, *in Edinburgh. The* EARL OF MORTON, LORDS RUTHVEN, HOME *and* LINDESAY, MAITLAND OF LETHINGTON, SIRS GEORGE *and* ARCHIBALD DOUGLAS, SIR JAMES BALFOUR, *and* KIRKALDY OF GRANGE *seated around a large table in consultation.*

MORTON. Well met, good friends; I think our course seems clear. In our chill climate, fruits take long to ripen, but still they do ripen, even if the sun shines out rarely. The sun has hitherto been clouded for our projects, but it appears to me, that at last, it has burst forth bright and warm. The Scottish masses are waking from the glamour that our lovely sovereign cast upon them. Her marriage with the Popish

Darnley sits ill on their Reformed stomachs, especially as it has been brought about by that hypocritic papal emissary, David Rizzio. To use the words of godly Master Knox, his stench is most unsavory in the nostrils of a nation, that has shown such hatred to the most dangerous enemy of our purified doctrine. Our own plan of action now must lie clear before us. In spite of the Queen's sudden passion for the bonnie long laddie, she has raised so high, even beside her in the highest seat, she now stoops to the base-born Italian lowness—

LINDESAY (*interrupting*). She covers him with wealth and dignities, and for the truckling low-born foreigner, robs us, the titled of the land. Every time I have to doff my bonnet to him—and we all must do it—it is hard to keep my dagger from her bosom. He usurps—

SIR GEORGE DOUGLAS. Do you remember, gentlemen, associates and friends, how when the nuptial ring was placed on the Queen's finger, the outlandish minion could not restrain his exultation, but in the very chapel shouted out, in monkish Latin, "Glory to God! It is done and cannot now be broken." How my blood boiled!

RUTHVEN. The Macedonian did not wait to untie the Gordian knot, but cut it with his sword, and the world still applauds the Greek's sagacity. There are swords as keen as his in Scotland, and daggers too, and men who know how to use both.

DOUGLAS. This case needs no gallant *Coup de Jarnac*, but rather the sly stick that Joab gave to Amasa, with "Art thou in health, my brother?" (*Laughs.*) It should be done to the Italian *a la Italiano!*

LETHINGTON. We have the trail, we need but follow it. Darnley's a dolt, and, what is more, the greater dolt, in that he's drunk with pride at his uplifting. And yet he is so common in his wantonness, and finds that women yield so quickly to his Royal suit, he deems all women of the same complexion. Could we arouse his jealousy? Remember Robert Bruce; and the Red Comyn, stabbed at the very altar.

KIRKALDY. Lethington, have you no thought of God, nor fear of Hell, to counsel thus!

LETH. Heaven! Hell!—Bogles to frighten children. My Laird of Grange, although you are a man of blood, a soldier, "a stout man, who always offers, by single combats and at the point of the sword, to maintain whatever you say;" and I a penman rather, I have as little a fear of what men dread the most as any belted earl or swordsman ever buckled on a breast-piece. Heaven and Hell are stories framed by priests and preachers to frighten children, not to scare grown men. *Your* conscience and your pride of orthodoxy will be your ruin. Pride must have a fall! I can read you without glasses. Your squeamishness will at some future time get you with all your conscience into a terrible scrape. You are not so cold, my Laird of Grange, that the warmth of Mary's glances has not already stricken home, clean through your polished cuirass.

KIRK. (*starting up, and laying his hand on his sword*). My Lord of Maitland!

MORT. Quarrelling, my lords, before the hunt's a foot! Give me money, women and authority, and I will not quarrel with the means by which I get them!

LETH. (*perfectly cool and without moving*). My Laird of Grange, your very heat betrays you. You are very like the good people of Laodicea, neither cold nor hot enough—Look to it! Lukewarm drinks set ill upon the stomach, and lukewarm people ever come to grief.

MORT. Peace! peace! my lords, we are forgetting Scotland and the holy cause we represent.

LETH. (*aside*). Hypocrites one and all; but I must pull each set of wires, so that my various puppets dance at the proper time to the piping I deem the fittest for the occasion and my purposes.

MORT. What are you muttering, Maitland?

LETH. Simply, Kirkaldy should be grateful, not irate. I but warn him! Has he forgotten Chastellar and Gordon? They loved Mary, and what came of it? The hangman's noose; the axe! My Laird of Grange, if Mary Stuart ever makes you love her, beware lest Cupid's knot turn into a halter to choke even you, the pink of chivalry.

KIRK. (*rises indignantly*). Maitland! do you dare to insinuate that I, Kirkaldy, am another maker (minstrel) or traitor. (MORTON *interposes*.)

MORT. Lords, this is no time for discord. Our country—well; not to feign, our interest—needs us, and we need ourselves in fittest mood for counsel and for action. (MORTON *crosses to* KIRKALDY, *and pacifies him*. LINDSAY *addresses* LETHINGTON, *in dumb-show, deprecating further irritation*.) Lethington speak! You are the coldest heart and subtlest head among us; what is your plan? My Laird of Grange, be patient!

KIRK. Patient! Ay, patient! My Laird of Maitland, you are—so says the general voice—a Roman philosopher, a stoic. Look to it yourself, lest you so entangle yourself in your own net you cannot extricate yourself with all your cunning ways. Although you may not fall upon your sword like the stoic-soldier, Cato, you may yet take a drink like Demosthenes, the Athenians' greatest orator, to save you from a worse than halter.

LETH. Well spoken, Laird of Grange. Now you have said your say and had your quip, and have shown your knowledge of the Humanities; now hearken to my plan. Mary, our gracious Queen, is but a woman after all, and brought up in a court where she learned more than prayers. She came to us heralded by stories of anything but fair

Lucretia's self control, and these have followed her. The holiest of our brethren still believe that Chastellar's head was cut off to keep his tongue from telling tales of how she lured him on and played with him and worse. This present favorite, Rizzio, is so high in her good graces that he is with her at all hours, day and night. Make Darnley once believe the Italian's had *his* rights and he will join us to make way with Davie. This will rouse the Queen—her Guisan blood. She is already disgusted, wearied with this boy-husband; his humors and his mistresses. Davie sent whither (*points upwards and then downwards*), who knows whither—Darnley must be disposed of. Mary then must have a lover bold, handsome, high in rank; one who, to possess the woman and to wed the queen, will stop at nothing and will venture everything. We must so manage it, that the new man will rid us of this Darnley; but, in the doing of the deed, so outrage public opinion that when Mary, carried away by passion, gives her hand to him, all Scotland will rise up like one man to drive him out and punish both.

MORT. A second Ahithophel!

DOUG. It is to be hoped that no Hushai will be found to traverse so goodly a plot.

KIRK. This seems like seething a kid in its mother's milk. And what of Murray? What will he say? Will he take part in this?

LETH. Yea and nay, not openly: but he will look at it approvingly betwixt his fingers.

(*All laugh again, and good humor is restored; all rise, consult together, and then, after exchanging opinions, resume their seats.*)

KIRK. But, my lords, this is all well enough for talk; but where will we find the man who will play our game, and yet be so chivalric in his disposition, so void of guile, so manly, and, even more and better for our projects, so filled with love of Mary, he will not see into the secrets of our Bond?

SERGEANT (*without below, at the entrance door of the dwelling*). Guard, turn out; stand to your arms! Ain High and Mighty Lord, the Earl of Bothwell! (*All rise and look at each other, as if seeking to divine each others thoughts.*)

LETH. (*smiling aside*). My leaven works!

USHER (*without, at the door of the apartment, and preparing to throw it open*). Ain High and Mighty Lord, the Earl of Bothwell!

(*All turn toward the door.*)

LETH. (*in a low tone, significantly*). Where is our man, my Lords? (*In a low voice.*) There is the very man! (*Pointing to the unclosing door.*) Here, now! (*The valves of the door are thrown wide open.*) Welcome! You come in time, my Lord of Bothwell!

(*All rise and greet* BOTHWELL *with effusion, who becomes the central figure of the Tableau as the Curtain falls.*)

Holyrood Palace.

ACT II.

SCENE I.—DARNLEY's *apartment in Holyrood Palace, beneath the famous room known to history as the Queen's Bedchamber. This scene should be so arranged that, when it opens (or rises), it will allow full space for a reproduction of* MARY's *Bedchamber and Cabinet or "Closet," in the rear of it, so that the latter (Scene II.) will be shown when Scene I. draws aside or opens, is drawn up or sinks.*

DARNLEY (*pacing nervously to and fro, stops every now and then as if expecting some one. His hands play with his dagger which, at intervals, he spasmodically, half-unsheathes and thrusts back again violently into its scabbard*). King and not king, husband and yet not head! She plays with me! Am I not her husband? Twice married, doubly in possession: handfasted, tried, accepted, married, crowned: and yet, what power have I? Murray is driven forth it is true, but he is ever present in his friends; cold, cruel Morton; sly, calculating Lethington, and all the rest, who have the people's ears; ay, and though John Knox possess the people's hearts. I am but a puppet, a toy, a cicisbeo, not as good! Then there's that wild fearless mosstrooper, stick-at-nothing Bothwell. I know not where he stands. I cannot comprehend it. Sometimes I think the Queen loves him, has loved him always, ever since he and I sought her in France, at Joinville, fifteen years ago. But let that pass. We will look to him hereafter. Rizzio's the present man; the knave, the sneaking cunning dog I trusted. The Virgin curse him! I'll have his blood before the midnight strikes; his heart's blood! He'll never thrust himself after to-night, between the Queen and me. Do I love her? I hate her now! Did I ever love her, or was it Scotland's crown and throne I coveted? Ha! Here is my chief reliance.

(*The clank of armor is heard without, and* RUTHVEN *enters. He wears a long loose gown, but under that, is clad in full panoply as if about to take the field, except as to his helmet, which he carries in his hand. A nightcap instead muffles his livid brow. He is deadly pale and walks with difficulty.*)

DARN. My Laird of Ruthven, you startle me: you look like a very bogle.

RUTHVEN. And nearly am one. Have I not arisen from a sore bed of sickness, to help in an act of justice due to my King and kingdom?

DARN. Justice! Yes, it is justice to put away the thing that stands between the King, nobility and husband, and owns both Queen and wife, the kingdom—all, all, all! Ever since that night I found the minion in the Queen's bed-chamber, and the door barred between my wife and me, my blood has been boiling with fever's heat and force. This night ends all. Be you all ready? I will have open the door and keep the Queen in talk till you come in. Remember, be alert, for only one man at a time is able to mount the narrow stairs. This night, shall it not end all, my lord?

RUTH. Assuredly, if your own courage is as hot and lasting as you say your fever-fit has been. But come, our friends await us, and the hour has struck on every bell that notes the time in Auld Reekie.

Exeunt.

SCENE II.—*The scene opens and discovers the famous cabinet within the bedchamber of Queen* MARY *in Holyrood Palace, so well known through pictures, descriptions* and photographs. The position of the characters should be arranged in exact accordance with the historical pictures.* QUEEN MARY *and* JANE, COUNTESS OF ARGYLE, *are at supper.* RIZZIO *is likewise seated near the table; his lute resting against his chair, as if he had been singing. The Queen sits in a double chair, of which one seat has been left unoccupied for* DARNLEY. BETON, ERSKINE *and* STANDEN *in attendance.*

MARY. Minstrel, resume your song: although it is not as joyous as becomes the theme.

---

* "The apartments (of Holyrood House) occupied (1822) by the Duke of Hamilton, fill the old portion of the Palace. On the second floor are those [once] occupied by Queen Mary, whose bed still remains. The furniture of this bed is of crimson damask, bordered with green silk tassels and fringes, and tradition assigns the decorations to

RIZZIO (*takes up his lute and sings to the accompaniment of this instrument*).

    You ask me what is love ? Oh, sweet !
    'Tis clothes, 'tis fire, 'tis drink, 'tis meat :
    'Tis anguish, rapture, life—'tis wings ;
    Of earthly happiness the springs !
    A crowd confus'd of hopes and fears,
    Of smiles and ecstacy and tears ;
    Of heaven on earth it gives the taste :
    And without love this orb 's a waste.
    Chaotic sphere like chilly moon ;
    A jangling rhythm without tune :
    Then grant me love or take me hence,
    For without love this life 's offence.

---

the fair hands of the unfortunate queen ; but the whole is now in a very decayed state. There are likewise some old chairs, covered with crimson velvet ; in this room a small opening is to be seen, which leads to a trap-stair ["a piece of wainscot, about a yard square, hangs upon hinges, opens on this trap-stair."—BREWERS' "*Various Palaces.*"] communicating with the apartment below. By this passage Darnley and his accomplices conveyed themselves into the CLOSET in which Mary was supping with her secretary, who was dragged out of the Closet through the Bedchamber into the Chamber-of-Presence, and there expired under repeated (56) blows."—"*Views in Edinburgh,*" 1822.

"QUEEN MARY'S BEDROOM.—A chamber twenty-two feet one inch, by eighteen feet six inches ; the ceiling divided into panelled compartments of diamond and hexagonal form, adorned with the emblems and initials of Scottish sovereigns ; and the walls are hung with tapestry, illustrative of the mythological tale of the Fall of Phæton.

  * * * Here stands, with fragments of the blankets, the bed of Queen Mary, the decayed hangings of which are of crimson damask, with green silk fringes and tassels, and the chairs and table, &c., are of the same period. The Queen's workbox is on the table at the bottom of the bed. The needlework represents Jacob's dream, and is said to have been worked by her own fair hands. The Baby-basket of James VI. is on the stand beyond the bed ; it was presented to Queen Mary by Queen Elizabeth on the birth of the Prince. *The door opposite on the right, half hidden by the tapestry, leads to the secret staircase by which* DARNLEY *and his infamous associates ascended to the royal apartments to assassinate* RIZZIO. *The one on the left leads to the little apartment so famous in Scottish Story* as the scene of the assault upon the unfortunate Italian, in the presence of the Queen. Every one whose imagination is at all vivid, will here easily realize the particulars of that terrible event ;—the Queen forcibly restrained by Darnley—the overthrown table and scattered viands—the fierce and scowling conspirators pressing into the little room—and the dagger left sticking in the body of Rizzio, who crouches behind Mary for protection. From this closet the assassins dragged their victim through the other royal apartments, stabbing him as they went, until he fell dead at their feet at the top of the staircase, by the door of the audience chamber. To this room the brutal Ruthven, reeking from the slaughter, returned and demanded a cup of wine ; and here probably it was that the conspirators threatened to cut the Queen "into collops" if she dared address the populace from the window."

REFRAIN.

Then grant me love or take me hence.
For without love this life's offence!

(*He gazes a moment on* MARY, *as if awaiting a responsive look, and receiving none, puts down his lute with a sigh and lapses into a revery.*)

MARY. Ah, Messire David, you are in a sad mood to-night. (*Takes the lute, tunes it, and sings to a rattling accompaniment*):

Love,* whence comes it and whither goes?
Love, how increaseth, chills to close;
Love, what is it? No one knows.

Love, who can explain it, its raptures and woes;
Love, true love, e'er stronger, e'er lovlier grows,
With the grace of the lily, and perfume of rose,
'Till hearts it has blended take long last repose.

Love, true love, 'tis body and soul,
And spirit combined in one exquisite whole,
And playing together, when perfect, one role.

There, that is music I like. But, hark! What do I hear?

BOTHWELL (*without and below*).

SERENADE.

Queen, soul, love, mine!
My first thoughts at waking, my last thoughts on sleeping,
When slumber is creeping, resistance o'er leaping,
Are thine and all thine.

Like moon in calm beauty, my vows all salute thee;
Thy beams on my slumbers, in rapture transmute me—
Ideas divine!

Like sun in his splendor, I waking adore thee;
Thy glories recalling, I prostrate implore thee
Be mine, ever mine!

All radiant with graces, thy inner lights lend thee.
In beauty perennial may blessings attend thee!
Be happiness thine!

* "L'Amour est, je ne scais quoi;
Qui vieut de je ne scais ou;
Qui finit je ne scais comment;
L'Amour vraie finit toujours en plus,"

Thy slave and thy lover, in constancy ever.
Let nothing the ties which unite us e're sever!
    May the ivy yet twine

Their fetters for both of us, loving and waiting;
Hope daily for both with new happiness freighting.
    Till at last thou 'rt mine!

For that I live dreaming, so eagerly dreaming—
The future, though distant, yet ever sure seeming.
    For thee still I pine!

DARNLEY (*enters from the private stair leading from his apartment, below, into the Queen's (his wife's) bedroom. MARY turns toward him with affectionate greeting. He sits beside her in the double chair. They kiss each other and embrace; he steals his arm about her waist and clasps her to him, as if they were on the best of terms.*)

MARY. My lord, have you supped? Shall I command another course for you? I thought you must have finished your supper by this time.

DARNLEY (*evasively*). I need no supper. Do not let me interrupt your meal. (*As he speaks the tapestry concealing the Secret Passage into the Queen's Bedroom is raised and RUTHVEN shows himself*).

MARY (*startled by the clash of his armor and ghastly appearance of RUTHVEN, whispers to DARNLEY*). What does this mean? Why comes this bold bad man; my mother's foe, my own? I thought he was dying. I meant to visit him, for although he is a murderer and a villain, he is the husband of my aunt. What means his naked sword? Is he distraught? Has he escaped his watchers and comes to me for safety, deeming himself pursued by the avenging ghost of his murdered victim, Charteris?

RUTHVEN (*who has seated himself while she has been whispering to DARNLEY*). I come here for your good.

MARY. Good? Do you look or act like one who comes for good?

RUTH. (*pointing at RIZZIO*). Yes, madam, for your good; to rid you of that minion. There is no harm intended to your grace, nor to any one, but to yonder poltroon, David.

MARY. What has he done?

RUTH. Ask the King, your husband.

MARY (*to DARNLEY, who has risen and is leaning on the back of her chair*). What means this?

DARN. (*faltering*). I know nothing of the matter.

MARY (*pointing to RUTHVEN*). Then away with him.

(THE LAIRD OF CREICH, ERSKINE, STANDEN *and attendants advance upon* RUTHVEN *to put him out; but he keeps them off with his sword.*)

RUTH. (*defending himself*). Lay no hands on me! I will not be handled.

(*As he is speaking the cabinet is invaded by Conspirators, who advance upon* RIZZIO *with menacing miens and threatening gestures. The* QUEEN *interposes herself in defence of* RIZZIO, *who draws his dagger which, manifestly, he has not the courage to use, and, falling on his knees, grasps the hem of her robe and hides his face in its folds.*)

MARY. What is the meaning of this? Do you seek my life?.

RUTH. (*making a pass with his sword at* RIZZIO). No, madam, but we will have out yonder villain, Davie. (MARY *seizes* RUTHVEN *by the wrist.*)

RIZZIO. Guistizia! Guistizia!

MARY. If my secretary, Signor Rizzio, had done anything amiss, the Lords of Parliament shall try him ; but the usual forms of justice shall be observed.

ANDREW KERR OF FAUDONSIDE. Here are the means of justice. (*Produces a rope with his left hand and with his right presents a dagg or pistol, which he presses against the bosom of the Queen, who confronts him intrepidly.*)

RIZ. (*speaking with great terror.*) I am a dead man.

MARY. Fear not, Signor Rizzio! The King will never suffer you to be slain in my presence; neither can he forget your faithful services. (DARNLEY *is abashed and about withdrawing.*)

RUTH. Sir, take the Queen, your wife and sovereign, to you. Pin her arms! Remove her!

(*Clamor without.* A Douglas! a Douglas! *Conspirators rush upon* RIZZIO ; *the table and chairs are overset, the* COUNTESS OF ARGYLE *seizes a candelabra as it is thrown down and saves the robes of the Queen from being enveloped in flames. For a moment all is dark: then followers of* MORTON *rush in with torches. A dreadful struggle ensues, all the conspirators striving to stab* RIZZIO, *who grovels at the Queen's feet, she still endeavoring to shield him.* RUTHVEN *seizes the Queen and throws her into the arms of* DARNLEY.)

RUTH. (*to the Queen*). Do not be frightened; there is no harm intended you. All that is done, is your husband's deed.

(MARY *struggles to free herself while in the arms of* DARNLEY.

RIZZIO, *grovelling at her feet and clinging to her dress, is crying, stammering and repeating,* Misericordia! Guistizia! Mercy! Madam, save my life! Guistizia!

MARY (*to* DARNLEY). Out upon you, dastard! You did come to betray me with a Judas kiss. You will live to remember this—your Judas kiss. (*To the Conspirators.*) Traitors and villains! Begone! or you shall suffer the law's severest penalties. I will protect this hapless creature, this innocent victim, this faithful servant, even although to him I owe this bitter moment, because that he won from my unwillingness a consent to wed the caitiff wretch now dares restrain his sovereign.

RUTH. This has lasted too long. Have out that gallant! (*indicating* RIZZIO).

DARN. Let him go, madam! They will not harm him!

RIZ. (*shrieking.*) Save my life, madam! Save my life, for God's dear sake!

GEORGE DOUGLAS (*snatching* DARNLEY'S *dagger from its sheath, and stabbing* RIZZIO *over the Queen's shoulder, leaving the dagger sticking in the wound*). This is the blow of the King!

KER. (*pressing his pistol against the Queen*). I will shoot you dead if you any longer struggle to save your minion.

MARY. Fire! If you do not respect the royal infant in my bosom.

DARNLEY (*pushes away* KERR'S *dagg or pistol, which misses fire, as* PATRICK BELLENDEN *makes a stab at the* QUEEN *with his rapier. The blow is parried with a torch by* ANTHONY STANDEN, *her page.* DARNLEY *forces the* QUEEN *down into a chair and holds her there while* RIZZIO *is torn away by the conspirators, and amid terrible uproar and oaths, clash of weapons, and attempts to slay him.*

RIZ. (*as he is hurried out*). Guistizia! guistizia!

(*Renewed and terrible uproar and cries without, then groans and cries of exultation, followed by a thumping sound as of a body thrown down stairs. The Conspirators gradually struggle back into the room, laughing and jesting with each other, wiping the blood from their weapons, and readjusing their garments.*)

RUTHVEN (*throwing himself, insolently, into a chair*). Give me a drink. Bring me a cup of wine: I am sore felled by my sickness.

MARY. Where is Messire David? Whither have they dragged him? Has he been put in ward, and where?

BEATOUN (*sadly*). Madam, it is useless to speak of David, as the man is dead.

MARY (*to* BEATOUN, *sorrowfully*). Dead? Ah, poor David, my good and faithful servant! May the Lord have mercy on your soul! (*To* DARNLEY, *savagely*). That was a Judas kiss.

(*A pause, grouping and tableau.* MARY *suddenly springs up and rushes to the window and throws it open, and shrieks for assistance. Through it is heard the clamor of an aroused populace and the clash of arms, and through the casement streams in the glare of torches carried by those without. Behind the scenes noise of fighting.*)

MARY. Help, help, my lieges! (DARNLEY *drags her away from the window.*)

RUTH. Madam, if you make such an outcry, sooner than these people should rive you from us, I would cut you into collops, and throw them down to the rabble.

MARY. Where can I look for aid?

(*Noise of fighting without, and cries:* Viva Bothwell! St. Bride for Bothwell! Spears and axes! Bothwell! Bothwell!

MARY (*falling into a chair*). Always faithful to his motto, "Klip trest!" My own brave Bothwell! I will trust him.

(*Through the main entrance to the chamber burst in the* EARLS OF BOTHWELL *and* HUNTLEY *with a body of serving and kitchen-men armed with spits, cleavers, knives and whatever weapons they could seize or came to hand. Their sudden inburst drives back the Conspirators and frees the* QUEEN. BOTHWELL *rushes to the* QUEEN, *who throws herself into his arms.*)

MARY (*to* DARNLEY). Ah! traitor and son of a traitor! Is this the recompense you give me, who have loaded you with benefits, and raised you to dignities so great and undeserved? Is this the reward you reserved for him who did so much for your good and honor? (*Wiping her streaming eyes.*) Ah! no more tears, but revenge! No more joy for me until your heart shall be as desolate as mine this night. I will now study revenge! (*Half swooning.*)

RUTH. (*sinking, overcome with faintness, into a chair*). A thousand devils! What have we here? Furies and hell! Curses on Maitland's policy and plan! We have slain the jackall here and let the lion go. Besotted fools, our work is all to do over again!

(*Behind the scenes.*) Long live the Earl of Bothwell!

(*The Conspirators prepare to renew the struggle,* BOTHWELL *confronting them triumphantly with the* QUEEN *in his arms.* DARNLEY *abashed contemplates the group, not knowing what to do. As the fighting is about to be renewed, the Curtain falls.*)

Edinburgh Castle.

ACT III.

SCENE I.—*Same as Act I., Scene I.* MARY *and* BOTHWELL *come forward from the arbor in amorous discourse*

MARY. Darling, the history of my loves is but a serial story of mishaps. Love, the sum total of a woman's life, has realized for me the verses of the Latin poet, that "love's a spring of delights, and afterward a season of despair." Dearest, you well know that I am versed in the Humanities, and most conversant with those poets, troubadours and versifiers of the affairs of the heart. Love, they say, is a mingling of honey and of acid, a "bitter-sweet." Mine has been indeed a bitter-sweet in which the former, bitterness, was the most potent. Yet no one will forego the sweetness of the entrance thereunto, even if the judgment doth assure the bitterness of the exit. It is indeed a most tempting bait that entices the poor fish to gorge its own destruction. My own Bothwell, young in years and in experience, I did love the boy Francis; but I had not then known you. I did lament him, but I had not as yet felt the first effects of the intense influence that your manliness, fidelity and mind exerted on my soul of souls. This varnished toy, this Darnley, and you came to me in my first months of sorrow. To whom did my heart cleave? To you! To whom did it incline at Joinville and at Jedburgh? To you, to you, to you!

BOTHWELL. And yet you allowed that traitor bastard, Murray, to drive me into exile.

MARY. Alas, my love, I am unpardonable, but (*bewitchingly in tone and manner*) I was powerless. That man, that betrayer, my father's son, was all powerful; and, weak as women always are when they should be strongest, I yielded. I am without excuse. State policy—

my curse upon the sad necessity—compelled the sovereign where the woman should have been all queen.

BOTH. I forgive that because I went, and the event proved all that I could wish. You were compelled to recall me. But you married Darnley.

MARY. The peace and stability of Scotland compelled me. The Queen of England drove me to the act. I was the tool of her accursed policy, the property of her ambition. You were in exile; woe is me that I consented to do so! I was without a friend to aid me. France, Spain, England, Rome, were providing me with husbands; Murray was depriving me of everything but the name of Queen. How, but by marriage, could I put a stop to the persecution on the one side, or have crushed the insolence of the other. Oh, my dear love, well you know that it was not then in my power to make choice of you, unless I would have been content, not only to have my crown torn from me, but also to resign both our lives to glut the implacable malice of our foes. I never loved this Darnley, and his ingratitude has made me hate him. Oh, my Bothwell, you must condone my wedding elsewhere than as my heart desired. I believe that in your heart, your wise and manly heart, you must now be perfectly convinced that there was an invincible necessity for this hated, hateful marriage, although the fury which filled your soul to behold me in another's arms would not permit you to acknowledge it. And yet, my own, my own dear Bothwell, my own dear life, I was, I am, I ever shall be yours and only yours.

BOTH. My own Mary, if this was and is so, where was that trust, you ever do protest, in me, when you, in spite of Darnley, made me your Lieutenant-General and, afterward, Warden of all Three Marches, an office never before held by one person:—ay, placed your Hepburn, omnipotent upon the Borders, as a barrier against England; and nathless, was afraid to call him to your aid against so many nearer but less dangerous enemies, you fear and feared.

MARY (*caressingly*). Not with you thus, here, by my side.

BOTH. Love of my youth, my manhood, and my prime; my truest life, my own Mary; you confess all this, and yet you gave yourself to him; this upstart, senseless, graceless, long-legged boy—more like a woman than a man: merely a lusty, beardless lady-faced Adonis; such as your astute uncle, the Cardinal of Lorraine wisely styled him, "a high-born quarrelsome coxcomb:" totally unmeet to be my own Mary's consort.

MARY. Think not, my Hepburn, it was love that furnished me with arguments to justify my choice of this ingrate caitiff, for I protest by that dread power, by which I have so often sworn, that Bothwell was the dearest thing on earth ; that he is so, and ever will be so while I have life.

BOTH. (*with a touch of sarcasm*). You bore with him full long, and it me seems that Hepburn and his loyalty were clean forgotten.

MARY. I married Darnley through policy's compulsion, not from choice. Surely the fire of true love never enkindled my affection for *him*. No time is pleasing to me that is not spent in giving you new demonstrations of my affection for you. Well may I err in the rules of government and state, when all my thoughts are taken up with love for you. If I had to choose whether to relinquish crown and state, or thee, my Bothwell, I would leave my dignity and kingdom to follow thee throughout the world, a simple damsel. I never deceived you and remit myself altogether to your will. Send me at any time advisement of what I shall do, and whatsoever may come of it, I will obey you.

BOTH. And say you so ? The time is come to prove it. Were you once free to love, not as now and in the past, in secret, but before the world, to wed, to crown, where would you be ?

(*As he utters these words and gesticulates, he spreads abroad his arms, questioning, and* MARY *throws herself into them.*)

MARY. Where would I be! Where my heart has been for many, so many years, my Bothwell ! Here ! here ! here !

BOTH. Then you do trust me now ?

MARY. Implicitly, my hero ; my knight, my MAN ! Do you think your Mary can ever forget the accomplished knight and fearless horseman who, at the Tournament near the Rood of Greenside, galloped in full panoply down the steep side of the Calton and leaped his steed into the ring, to the terror and admiration, not only of his Queen, but of her whole Court ? You seemed that day the god of war, in grace, incarnate !

BOTH. Then let us in. (*Pointing to the arbor in the background.*) The sun is near his setting. Night, which brings counsel as a rule; this night will bring release and usurp the privilege of day. All is prepared as planned with your consent, assistance, wishes and commands. There let us rest awhile in fond commune and with your kisses seal firm the bond hereafter makes us one—forever one.

(*He uncloses his embrace after kissing her passionately, and then, with his arms thrown about her neck and hers twined around his waist, they disappear in the arbor, whispering fondly as they go.*)

BOTH. (*within the bosket, sings*):

    Mary, my Queen !
    When banished from thy presence dear,
    The world seems desolate and leer,
        And steeped in gloom :

My actions spectral movements seem,
I do not live, but idly dream;
   The world's a tomb,
Till, at thy coming, light and life,
With beauty, grace, and glory rife,
   My thoughts illume.

What, then, to me is Scotland's ban?
My soul dilates, once more a man,
   The world I dare;
For thee I live, for thee would die—
Yea, for one glance of thy fond eye,
   And nothing care;
Beside thee smiling, all is light;
Absent from thee, the world is night,
   Mary, my Queen!
         (*Scene changes, or opens.*)

SCENE II.—*Interior of the notorious building in Edinburgh, known as the Kirk-o-Field.* Time, night of 9th–10th February,* 1567.

As the space between the stage and the arch over it is very lofty, and the actual rooms represented had very low ceilings, there must be a double flooring, showing DARNLEY'S *sleeping apartment over Queen Mary's room, in the latter of which the powder (with which the building was blown up) was stored, under* DARNLEY'S *bedchamber.*

Upper Stage (U. S.) *signifies* DARNLEY'S *bedchamber. Lower Stage* (L. S.) QUEEN MARY'S *room.*

In the apartment (U. S.) DARNLEY *is discovered reading, in company with his body-servant or page,* TAYLOR.

QUEEN MARY, BOTHWELL, *the Conspirators,* cum suis, *first show themselves on the stage below and afterward mount a staircase to the Left Side facing the audience. The commencement of this staircase might be shown laterally, so that the course of their ascent would be recognized by the audience and nevertheless leave the whole of the upper portion of the upper stage clear for the action of the piece.*

L. S. *Enter* MARY *with her train, and the Conspirators, Nobles with Attendants, lighting them with flambeaux or torches, and* BOTHWELL *following. He is richly but soberly attired.*

---

* KIRK-O-FIELD.—The house of Kirk-o-Field, as Buchanan, the literary organ of the conspirators, declared, "was the most unwholesome, horrible and dangerous place to which an invalid could be brought."   *   *   *   It was not. "The contrary has

BOTHWELL (*approaching* MARY *to the front, leaving the rest in the background*). The passion kindled in my bosom sixteen years, since when first we met at Joinville, in the sunny land of France, when my "White queen" was widow, the widow of a boy, who, with all his fondness, could never fill the soul of one fit for a Cæsar's mate. For sixteen years this passion has fed upon my heart, nourished by hope and faith. My love was like the morning sun, obscured by mists and clouds; it was felt, not seen. But when at my lone headquarters at the Hermitage, you deigned to visit your poor wounded knight, it seemed as if the mists and clouds all fled. Then followed your sojourn at Glasgow. Your letters by French Paris assured me I had won the game on which I had staked my life. And now the sun has attained meridian height. Will it shine out and in splendor? This night the blow will be struck which shall decide whether that sun shall stand still in full noontide blaze, as it stood still at Joshua's command on Gibeon, or sink in storm and ruin. Thou hast said and writ, that thou art all my own. When the crack comes which sends hence this unruly boy, wilt thou stand to it. The only obstacle is thus removed and if thy purpose holds, then, then thou art mine, before the world, as thou hast

---

since been demonstrated by the Medical Faculty of Edinburgh uniting in choosing it for the site of the Royal Infirmary; in fact, the ground is at present occupied by the College. The Thief's Row * * * was neither more nor less than the Sanctuary of our Lady's Kirk-o-Field, which remained, like that attached to the Abbey of Holyrood, long after the dissolution of its monastic foundation. Whatever might be said of the badness of such a neighborhood, applied no less to the Edinburgh Palace of the Regent Hamilton, where his brother, the Primate of Scotland, was then residing within sight and hearing of everything going on in the lodgings chosen for Darnley. The Mansion itself was a substantially built edifice only two stories high, with a basement or cellar which served for the kitchen and offices.

A spiral staircase in a turret, defended by what was then called, and is still called in Scotland, a turnpike, on the same plan as a wicket turnstile, communicated with the private entrance through a low postern-door in the Town-Wall, and gave access to both chambers through their respective lobbies. Behind these were the small apartments called *garderobes*, in which the attendants slept; and considering the fact that no less than five perished with Darnley, and that one absented himself that night, and another was taken out alive, they must have been strangely crowded.

Scotch dormitories were, however, arranged for persons of inferior rank very much in the manner of berths in a steam-packet, in recesses in the walls, masked with sliding panels, of which many examples may still be seen in ancient castles, as well as the Highlands hotels and cottages." STRICKLAND'S "*Mary Stuart*," I. 386.

See "Murray's Handbook for Scotland," 58 (2): "Kirk of Field lay almost due east by south of Edinburgh Castle, about half a mile; and a little more than that west by south of Holyrood Palace. Drummond street, leading out of South Bridge opposite the College, occupies in part the site of *The Kirk-o-Field*, in which stood the house occupied by Darnley, which was blown up, *with him in it*, as was generally but erroneously supposed. 9th—10th February, 1567."

long been mine in secret, and as I have been wholly thine since the first hour we met.

MARY (*looking round upon her suite and finding that they are absorbed in conversation, and not observing her*). All that I wrote from Glasgow and spoke, even this very evening in the palace garden, I felt and feel. There's not a thought I placed on paper and sent thee by French Paris, but that I felt and feel. Take thou the hand that held the pen and try my pulse! Does it beat calmly?

BOTH. (*after taking her hand and holding it a minute*). Like clockwork. Like the tides obedient to the laws that never change; strong, full and regular.

MARY. So holds my purpose. Is everything prepared?

BOTH. Even beyond our hopes. These Lairds with whom I hold this Bond are neither true to thee nor me; but faithful to themselves; yea, they are fiercely true to their own common interests, as is the love that fills our souls for each other. Darnley this night must die! Even though the whole powder-plot should fail, he dies as surely as if an earthquake were to heave and split the soil, and swallow up these walls and all within them. There is not an enemy he ever made but circles it in arms; and the few servitors that feed and fill the mine are nothing to the numbers who compass Kirk-o-Field without. Fear nothing! If all the powder I have brought from Dunbar should but suffice to lift the roof, there is enough of it stored beneath the very walls' foundations to send them soaring.

MARY. How? You amaze me!

BOTH. This Bond, distrusting Bothwell's courage, has made their vengeance "sicker," and plotting with me have plotted against thee and me and Darnley, that their vengeance fail not. Not only he and his, but the very stones of Kirk-o-Field will kiss the stars to-night if there's virtue in saltpetre.

MARY. My own, my own true knight; my Bothwell! But, hark! Our conversation has lasted long enough. We understand each other. I leave early, soon, thou knowest, to grace Sebastian's wedding at the palace. A few short sweetened words to lull this man's distrust and I will forth. Then see thou to it! Be wary! Let no suspicion light on thee—nor me; but— FAIL NOT!

Queen MARY, *and her suite, likewise, and* BOTHWELL *leave* (L. S.), *ascend the stairs, and enter* DARNLEY'S *chamber* (U. S.). *The Attendants with torches exeunt, withdrawing to one side.*

The action (U. S.) *for the most part, is in dumb show: the Nobles paying their court to* DARNLEY; MARY, *apparently, conversing affectionately with him.*

L. S. *As soon as* MARY *and the others are thus occupied* U. S., *enter from the rear, through the postern,* BOTHWELL's *followers,* HUBERT ORMISTON *and* HAY OF TALLA, *bearing sacks of powder.* HUBERT *or* FRENCH PARIS *lighting them with a candle.*

U. S. BOTHWELL *suddenly leaves* U. S. *and descends by the stairs to* L. S.

BOTH. (*to his followers*). My heavens, what a din ye make! They may hear above all ye do. And how you look, Hubert! all be-smirched with powder! Heard ye not what the Queen said when she saw you? "Mercy, Paris, how begrimed you are." Wash your face and hands and look innocent, if you have pluck enough. (*In a low tone communing with himself.*) Most curious coincidence! Like the pale horse of the fourth seal in Revelations: the White Steed of Death transported hither from Dunbar, the fatal sacks will send Lord Darnley up—or down—which way he goes it matters not, so that he goes.

(*The attendants signify obedience to* BOTHWELL's *warning and having concealed the powder with tapestry and the hangings of the bed, go out* (L. S.) *through the postern.* BOTHWELL *re-ascends to* DARNLEY's *apartment* U. S.

U. S. DARNLEY (*Evidently pleading with the Queen*). My queen! my wife! desert me not! Let us once more be one, as erst we were; one table, one bed, one life. Grant this, oh! sovereign lady, or your poor Henry doth not desire ever to leave this room a healthy man again. Oh! be once more my loving bride of Weymiss and of Stirling, and I will go wherever you do list. Let us be as in our better days, before I sinned, together at bed and board, and live like wife and husband!

(FRENCH PARIS *shows himself, unseen by* DARNLEY, *at entrance door* (U. S.), *signalling that all is ready.* MARY *makes a sign, that she understands.*)

MARY (*kissing* DARNLEY, *and placing a ring on his finger; with a smile*). Sweet, you are an invalid! You are nervous! You are fearful! There is no recipe against fear. It is time you were abed (*distant bells toll eleven*). Eleven is striking. It is later than I thought. I must not break my promise to Bastian and his bride. My lords and gentlemen, see that the torches are lighted. I will return on foot.

(BOTHWELL *and the Queen's suite quit the apartment* U. S., *descend the stairs and leave the house* L. S. *Through the open door by which they go out flashes in the glare of the flambeaux or torches, as they are lighted.*)

U. S. MARY (*throwing her arms around* DARNLEY's *neck*). Good night, sweet! We will see more of each other hereafter. (*Kisses him, then, aside.*) Kiss for kiss. You kissed me as the signal for poor Davie's murder: I kiss you as the signal of my revenge and my emancipation. Kiss for kiss!

DARN. (*with his arms around her waist, strives to detain her ; she unclasps his hands and gently places him in his chair, and throwing kisses at him as she goes, draws near the door at the head of the stairs,* U. S., *stops, and then with a changed demeanor, and with emphasis, addresses* DARNLEY.

MARY (*significantly*). This time last year, and about this hour—poor David Rizzio was murdered. (*With the last words she passes through the door* U. S., *and descends to* L. S. TAYLOR *lighting her down the stairs. She goes out through the main entrance, left side,* TAYLOR *closes and locks the door.* L. S , *after her ; then goes into the Queen's bedroom, and tries the postern* (L. S. *rear.*) *Assured that it is locked, he passes out of the door opening upon the entry, locks it* (L. S.), *ascends the stairs to* U. S. *and rejoins* DARNLEY, U. S., *who has started up from his chair as the Queen spoke her last words and continued, while* TAYLOR *is absent. gazing at the door as if absorbed in reflection upon what the Queen had said.*)

DARN. (*to* TAYLOR, *as he enters*). Heard you what her Majesty said on leaving.

TAYLOR. I did my Lord. The words were ominous. It is just eleven months to-night since Signor Rizzio was slain.

DARN. Those words were like a black bull's severed head, portending sudden, violent death or murder, here in Scotland. They seemed to drip blood on my ears, as they fell from her lips, even as she kissed me. My soul is sad within me! Oh! I remember! I remember! Mine was a Judas kiss, that night. Such was her declaration after the plot revealed itself in blood, and Rizzio was dead. (*Wringing his hands.* A Judas kiss—then—that it was. Oh! I repent me! Was her kiss to-night another Judas kiss ? Woe is me! Why do I recall this, at this moment? (*Prays silently.*)

TAY. Take courage, my good lord; the Queen may not have intended anything. Her words may have been an accidental freak of memory.

DARN. (*not attending to* TAYLOR'S *attempt at comfort*). What did she mean? What could she have meant? And, yet, she was so kind. (*Looking at the ring* MARY *had given him.*) And gave me this, and promised to return and give me more of her good company henceforth—and yet those words. They sounded like a menace. It likes me not. (*Seating himself.*) Draw the table hither, and trim the lamp! Bring the Breviary, and read the Fifty-fifth Psalm. I cannot sleep. Those words have banished sleep.

TAY. (*obeys, brings a book,* DARNLEY *settles himself into an attitude of listening and* TAYLOR *proceeds to read in a low voice, inaudible to the audience. Dumb show.*)

L. S. *While this action is going on* U. S., *the postern* (L. S.) *is unlocked, and* FRENCH PARIS *enters with a smaller bag of powder, unties it, and lays a train from the bed to near the door, and finally adjusts to it a piece of lunt,* (*slow-match*). *Simultaneously* BOTHWELL *appears at the door, with a slouched hat drawn over his face and draped in a trooper's cloak, watching the proceedings. Behind him, looking over his shoulder, stand* HEPBURN, ORMISTON *and* HAY OF TALLA. FRENCH PARIS *lights the slow-match, goes out of postern hurriedly, closes and locks the door. The slow-match flickers, sputters, but does not burn.*

U. S. DARNLEY (*starting up suddenly*). Heard you no noise below?

TAY. (*after listening*). None, my dear Lord.

DARN. I am so nervous, so unmanned, so weak from sickness and faint-heartedness. I must go forth into the garden to breathe one breath of the fresh air.

TAY. You will catch your death of cold, my Lord!

DARN. (*forcing* TAYLOR *aside, who tries in vain to detain him*). I'd rather die a thousand deaths of cold without, than freeze to death with terror here within. (*He thrusts* TAYLOR *aside violently, catches up a furred cloak, and followed by* TAYLOR *rushes through the door* (U. S. *left*), *springs down the stairs, opens the main entrance door, left side, and flies out.*

As they disappear (L. S., *rear*).

BOTH. (*without*). I have watched the match through the key-hole It does not burn. Unlock the door! Let me go in and see to it.

(*Sound of struggling without.*)

FRENCH PARIS (*without*). Oh, go not in, my Lord! Oh, go not in! Tempt not your fate, my Lord! You will perish! Have patience, my dear Lord; for the Queen's sake, have patience! If not for your own sake, for the Queen's sake forbear!

All is now quiet without and within—a pause of a few minutes—suddenly the slow-match flares up; kindles the train; the fire runs across the room; the powder explodes; the house blows up and falls in ruins, and through the shattered rear (representing the outer wall of the house) are seen the corpses of DARNLEY *and* TAYLOR, *strangled, lying dead on a sort of terrace, so as to be distinctly visible from the front. View of Edinburgh and Arthur's Seat in the distance. Immediate clangor of bells and cries of the alarmed neighborhood. Amid the uproar the voice of* SIR ARCHIBALD DOUGLAS, *at the extreme rear, is distinctly heard.*

BALFOUR. Eternal good night to my Lord Darnley! The deed is done, and well done!

As the smoke drifts away, the din without increases; other bells ringing alarm, join in amid the deafening clangor. Curtain falls.

Bothwell Castle.

ACT IV.

SCENE I.—*An Apartment of the Suite occupied by the* EARL OF MURRAY, *in Edinburgh. Date, 8th April,* 1567.

The curtain rises upon MURRAY, *in earnest discourse with* MORTON *and* LETHINGTON, *discussing the affairs of Scotland.*

MURRAY. It grieves me sorely to find myself all powerless to avert such evils from my country ; to see my sister falling completely in the snares of such a man as Hepburn, the profligate, the simple sworder and however brave—no man can deny his valiantness—so utterly devoid of principles we follow as our guides.

MORTON. Murray, between us, who understand each other thoroughly, what need is there of empty words. It is with us as with the old Roman augurs ; they could scarcely look each other in the face without laughing. Such utterances as yours, my lord, are giff-gaff. Your goal is supreme power. You thirst, you hunger, languish for the crown, or at least the sovereign authority denied by birth, by accident. You talk too much and are too squeamish. You do not object to eat the cosset when the butcher has dressed it for your table; but shrink yourself from killing it or even standing by to see the butcher slay and flay it. You talk too much. When we had kept your skirts all clean and clear of Rizzio's taking off, so that the poor thing, your sister, verily believed you innocent of blame, and claimed your sympathy, and gave you her confidence, you needs must talk and over-act the part. Again, when Darnley was blown up and opportunely, and your noble countess was taken sick and summoned you to her side, you needs must talk anew, and the whole country rung with words you dropped in going to her. What was repeated showed you were all privy to the plot. Away to France. We made short work with Rizzio and with but little space got rid of Darnley. Set off for France! Leave all to Lethington and me! This man, this Bothwell, has not risen so high, but that we can fly a hawk will bring him down. He is too honest. He thinks he can rule without a party. No man ever could do that; rule by sheer force of will, of loyalty. He dreams that devotion to his country, to Scotland, "Land o' the Leal," and his still stronger passion for the Queen, are all that is needed.

MUR. Bad as they say we are, I must admit (*laughing slyly*) that among our *blackguards* Bothwell is that *rara avis*, a *white* crow, a miracle of virtue.

MOR. Make no delay, blindfold the Queen! Never was woman so ductile in the hands of anyone can play on her affections; so easily cajoled. Consign your only child, your daughter, to her wardship, and remit to her best offices your countess! This will be a blind. This very trust will allay all her suspicions.

MUR. But, meanwhile, you take no count of Bothwell. Maitland, my Lord of Morton, seems too sanguine.

LETHINGTON. Bothwell's sun is soaring to its noon. Never a sun arose that did not have a setting, some sooner and some later. The days are short in Scotland, except in summer, and summer's not yet come. As yet 'tis early spring, with weather most uncertain. The coming summer must be all ours with its long days and longer twilights. Before the summer solstice, Bothwell's day will have been swallowed up by night. The game is ours. We hold the winning cards. (*Significantly*) I hold the ace of trumps?

MUR. (*eagerly*). The ace of trumps? How? Who?

LETH. Kirkaldy, Laird of Grange.

MUR. Kirkaldy?

LETH. Ay; you seem astonished. You do not note the setting of the wind as does an eye, like mine, that is ever fixed upon the vane of popular opinion and circumstances. Kirkaldy is a mere soldier; a good one, it is true, but nothing more. His head is not well balanced, and his heart impressionable. Already he casts sheep's-eyes upon your sister, and she returns his gaze with sympathetic glances. Poor woman, I would pity her did she not stand between us and our fortunes; but pity is too precious a commodity to throw away. I admit that she loves Bothwell with all the passionate ardor of her double nature. She comes by it honestly. She has it from her father, the late king, who gave so many noble sprouts to Scotland; and from a mother, the woman of Lorraine, the Guise. And, more, report assigns to her prime favorite, the gay gallant, gracious Cardinal Beatoun, the authorship of Mary Stuart. Mary herself, although so dead in love with Bothwell, that she denied long since no proofs of it; long, long before we recognized the fact; yes, loved him back into the days when she wore weeds for Francis—nathless, she had an eye meanwhile for others; Damville, Chastelard, John Gordon; nay she went so far as to handfast and then wed Darnley; loving this Bothwell all the time. She is a born coquette; not bad, but easily twisted around a subtle finger. Leave all to us, to me! Kirkaldy is my ace of trumps! As Morton says, "Away to London, to Elizabeth, to France : be patient : bide the time!"

James Stuart, Earl of Moray.

MUR. (*who has listened attentively and reflectively, and marked the drift of all these arguments*). My mails are all prepared. Keep me advised! My amplest influence and most puissant backing you have —may use them to the uttermost; but save appearances. Keep me clear from blame, and, if I grasp the sceptre, rest assured we will divide. Farewell. (*Exit.*)

LETH. (*as* MURRAY *goes out*). God speed! (*To* MORTON, *who has latterly remained somewhat in the background; silent, but intent on every word that passes*). Divide! Yes, that we will, or your proud day, my Earl of Murray, will be as short as Darnley's was, as Bothwell's shall be. (*Extending his hand to* MORTON, *who grasps and shakes it assentingly.*) Now, for Kirkaldy! to plume the popinjay, and set him up, so that his vivid colors shall attract our bird's attention.* Then, with dulcet piping on our part, all safely hid, we'll tole her into the trap we have set. After that, when Mary's taken, *away* with the popinjay; into the dust heap with him! I must follow Murray, to get him off for London and to France; our work brooks no delay. (*Exit.*)

* Here the question suggests itself, Why did Mary permit herself to be deluded by Kirkaldy? Was she, like many women of her class, suddenly overcome by a wild spasm of passion for him—one of those outbreaks which Bothwell so greatly feared after his marriage with her, and against which he guarded her and his honor with the ultra suspicious jealousy of a Spaniard; or did she believe, as the celebrated English historian Lord Mahon, expresses it, "No one, perhaps, except the immovable Knox, was able to bear up against them [her charms?] Her transcendant beauty [?] was joined to the most bewitching manners, and few even of her bitterest enemies could help doing homage to the mastery which she thus exerted over the hearts of men."

"But her mental gifts were still more remarkable. Acuteness, grasp, readiness, and fertility of resource were all characteristic of her intellect. The subtlest statesman could not circumvent her. The most practised reasoners failed to get the better of her in discussion. Menace could not daunt, danger rather inspirited her. We have said that Knox was invulnerable to the graces of her person and the witchery of her manners; but it is plain, even from his own reports of interviews which took place between them, that he was no match for her in argument. The greatest of English queens was her contemporary, and in some respects her rival, but even Elizabeth's genius looks pale when confronted with the brilliancy of Mary's. *She seemed indeed born to rule the world, and had her self-control been at all proportionate to her courage, her talent, and her beauty*, she would in all probability have accomplished results in her day that must have had an enduring influence upon the destinies of Europe. BUT THE STRENGTH OF HER PASSIONS RUINED ALL. ☞ "*Combined with her penetrating intellect and her noble physique, there was an emotional nature as ardent as it was unscrupulous.* ◄

"It is when we take all these elements into consideration, and view her conduct in the light of them, that alone we have any chance of dispelling the almost enigmatic obscurity which has appeared so long to surround her history."

"At the bar of impartial justice, Mary Stuart stands convicted of having been 'Act and Part' in the murder of her husband, Darnley.

"As to the other point of her having acted under the influence of *a guilty attachment* to Bothwell, *there is still less room for hesitation*. Let any one only read over that Apology for her marriage, which she transmitted to the Guises of France, and it must be obvious how painfully she flounders between truth and falsehood. Everything, indeed, points to the same conclusion. That most unseemly visit of hers to Bothwell, at his Castle of Hermitage; that mockery of justice by which he was acquitted of having any share in the murder of Darnley; that ABSURD STORY of the Queen's ravishment, which it is impossible for any candid reader to peruse without seeing that, like Horace's girl, the Queen was but *male pertinax* in the matter; those passionate expressions which she uttered of her determination to cling to Bothwell, even after it was clear that to do so would prove her ruin, all lead to the same conclusion—that

Mor. (*looking after him with a subdued cunning laugh*). Am I alone of iron; as Murray often saith, impenetrable? Am I the only Lord in Scotland that is proof against this Mary Stuart? And yet, it seems to be so. Little does Maitland dream that I see through him as through all the rest. Away, Earl Murray! Justly, Maitland looks beyond, and thinks that as he rolls each stone up, slowly or swiftly, but ever surely, to the edge of the beetling crag, that he can topple over each in turn and, then, at last, Mary remains queen, with Maitland, her Prime Minister. He

James Douglas, Fourth Earl of Morton.

counts without his host. Morton will hold over. Morton, who knows no love nor lure but interest. When Kirkaldy has served Murray's turn

---

she was laboring under *an almost insane passion* for the worthless profligate." (Why use such terms of the "great Earl"? Was he worse than his peers? No! Was he as bad? No! Was he far better? Yes. He was honest, loyal and intrepid.

It is quite needless to call in, for the decision of this question, the famous Casket Letters. These may or may not be genuine. *We have no doubt ourselves as to the verdict which should be returned regarding them.* But our purpose is already accomplished without their aid. *The guilt of Mary, is to our mind clear as any proposition in Euclid,* and the *bona fides* of Buchanan is vindicated. That there may not be errors, extravagances and exaggerations in his "*Detectio*," we do not maintain. These are in-

and Lethington his own, as he supposes, in truth mine, he too must go and Morton reign as Regent nominally ; in fact, with England's backing, as dictator, King in all but name, supreme.   (*Scene changes.*)

(*A lapse of eleven days* is supposed to occur between this Scene and Scene* II.)

SCENE II.—*The interior of the famous "Annesley Tavern" in Edinburgh, after the termination of the historic "Ainslie Supper." Time, after midnight,* 19*th*-20*th April,* 1567. *Visible evidences, to the rear of the stage, that a grand banquet is just concluded. The wax candles in the candelabra have guttered away or burnt down. A long disordered table is strewn with the relics of a feast ; goblets and flagons upset upon the table, around which appear many chairs and stools, some still upon their legs and others overturned. Several of the guests, overcome with wine, are being helped or carried out by attendants, others are being cloaked. Cries are heard without summoning the horses and suites of noted guests.* BOTHWELL, HUNTLEY, MORTON, LETHINGTON *and others stand apart, talking over what has occurred.*

BOTHWELL *and* HUNTLEY *disengage themselves from the groups and come forward ; the rest go out by the rear door.*

BOTHWELL. You must admit, my brother, that never was a ticklish piece of business better managed. With all my hopes and strong abiding faith, I scarcely could have counted on such an unanimity. Why all signed willingly, except that sneaking Eglinton, who stole away so quietly, he disappeared like a very wraith. Here I hold the Bond (*showing a roll of parchment*) signed by at least five bishops, the bastard, Murray, nine earls and seven lords of little less account, among the high nobility, papists and protestants alike, counselling and urging the Queen to marry me. It sets forth that she cannot find throughout the world a nobler or more fitting mate, endowed

---

cident to all men who write as near as he did to the date at which the events recorded actually took place. But his substantial accuracy is established, and however much our romantic or sentimental feelings may be wounded, *we must, in deference to historical fact, admit that the beautiful* QUEEN MARY *was, in reality,* ONE OF THE MOST ABANDONED AND UNSCRUPULOUS OF HER SEX."

* In order to indicate the intervals, the longer or more important lapses of time between the Scenes in Acts IV. and V., it might be advisable to drop an inter-act curtain, as Irving does, at the end of Act II of his adaptation of "The Merchant of Venice," after the elopement of Jessica and Lorenzo, and lift it again to exhibit the return of Shylock to his desolate home.

with all the qualities most proper for the station. By it they pledge their lives, their fortunes, and their honors to sustain and maintain the marriage and its consequence, *fas et nefas:* nay, what is more and stronger, therein they invoke upon their souls the stigma of being accounted unworthy and faithless traitors, neither worthy of reputation nor credit at any time thereafter, if they violate their pledges as signed by them (*pointing to the signatures on the Bond or roll he holds*). Never in Scotland was there signed a stronger Bond, or one of which the intention was more clearly manifest. Is it not so?

HUNTLEY. Assuredly, you have the adhesion of the major part of the most powerful peers and strongest hands and intellects in Scotland.

BOTH. (*unrolling the parchment and pointing to the leading signature*). And, see, my old enemy, James Stuart, leads the roll. It is true he was not present, but that is in keeping with his cautious character. I hardly thought he would sign, but his second self, his Machiavel, that arch devil, Morton, or the Chameleon, Lethington, cajoled or coaxed him into it. However, I ought not to be so much surprised after all, recalling that after Darnley was sent so opportunely to his appropriate place—even before I was acquitted of all art and part in the grim work: and while the miserable rabble of the capital and so many of the better classes of the burghers were wildest in their underhand as well as open accusations against the Queen and myself—he had the courage to give me a grand banquet in his lodgings, to testify his full belief in his royal sister's innocence and in my own, of any participation in the death of that unfledged booby and bustard with fine legs.

HUNT. Ay, and thereby to the world gave best assurance that he, at all events, was certain that you, my dear Bothwell, was entirely free from guilt.

BOTH. (*with a quiet laugh*). Considering that in intention and in everything, save that his hands were neither black with powder nor red with blood, the 'bastard' was as guilty as any one of us. I had a right at least to thus much countenance and backing. He is a sneaking dog, who aye makes his fangs meet in the leg behind when the wolf is close beset in front; but never flies at the throat, unless the rest of the pack have crippled the quarry. Huntley, you must confess, and you have reason to do so, that he is a dangerous—if but a sneaking tyke.

HUNT. Much as you have occasion to hate Murray for the past, how much more I; my race's ruin, my father's death, my brother's judicial murder; all, all were due to him. To you I owe my rehabilitation; my life can scarcely pay the debt. (*Extending his hand, which* BOTHWELL *grasps with fervor.*) In life and death I am yours: command me.

BOTH. Brother, I am right glad that of your own accord and without any solicitation you speak so strongly. Can I count on you?

HUNT. (*raising his right hand, as if affirming what he says*). I repeat, command me! Simply express your wishes, and what you wish is as good as done.

BOTH. (*again exhibiting the roll of parchment that he holds*). You see this Bond! It recommends me as the most proper husband for the Queen; although I am a married man and my wife is your sister. I must be divorced. The Queen desires, Scotland needs the sacrifice. It is a hard condition, but let your sister Jane consent and I will endow her richly for the future. The Barony of Haddington and all its ample revenues shall be assigned to her and hers forever. As for you, the House of Gordon shall be most richly recompensed and lift its noble head as rich in land and appanage as in its palmiest days.

HUNT. (*after a thoughtful pause, then sadly but firmly*.) These are hard lines, James Hepburn; but I consent. Your marriage with the Queen has now become an absolute necessity for her, for you, for Scotland; ay, for me, and necessity knows no law. Again, I repeat (*giving his hand to* BOTHWELL), for life, for death, command me! Now, what more?

BOTH. Delay is our worst enemy. Nowadays things move fast and every hour lost is pregnant with peril and augmenting difficulties. The next step is to publicly gain possession of the Queen's person. This must be done through the semblance of a ravishment. She has consented; she is all ready to hoodwink the good people. I must carry her off to my grim Castle of Dunbar. After she has been there, alone with me, you understand me, Huntley, for some half a score of days or so, and in my power absolute, with her consent, connivance and full will, she must wed me (*significantly*) to save what little reputation she has left. In fact the thing stands so there is no time to lose, even to save what little credit has been left her by Murray, Morton, Maitland and their crew.

HUNT. (*starting*). What do you mean?

BOTH. The answer must be spoken *in* your ear, so that no second ear can catch it. (*He whispers a few words to* HUNTLEY, *who by gestures expresses the greatest astonishment.*)

HUNT. (*with bated breath, stammering.*) What! What? By you?

BOTH. (*lays his fingers on his lips*). You now understand that any delay is impossible.

HUNT. (*shaking his head*). No, no; indeed no!

BOTH. Now off with you, you most astonished man. Make all your preparations and your moves in strict accordance with the plans that I here give you. (*Takes two folded papers from the bosom of his doublet, and hands them to* HUNTLEY.) The smallest is for you. Deliver the second, largest, to the Queen. After she reads it, let me have due answer as fast as horse and man can bring it. Keep me advised from time to time. I have ever lived up to the fullest meaning of the motto of my house, "Kiip trest!" Be faithful! I will be ready! See that you get a good ready likewise! Now, good-night. After all this, are you with me?

HUNT. Again I repeat, command me! I am yours for life, for death. (*As he speaks these words, he half draws his sword from its scabbard and thrusts it in with an audible snap, as if to accentuate his words.*) For life, for death! Good-night.

BOTH. Good-night, my brother! God be with you! Good-night!

HUNTLEY *goes out by the main door in the rear;* BOTHWELL *stands lost in thought for a moment, then brings his hands together with a loud clap, as if perfectly satisfied, and leaves the room by a side door.*

The scene (III.) closes in front of the banquet table and disorder in the rear, so as to allow ample time to clear the stage, behind, during the succeeding Scene III.

Between Scenes II. and III. about four days are supposed to elapse. The other intervals between the following scenes can be intimated by the dropping of an interlude curtain.

SCENE III.—*At the Fountain- or Almond-Bridge (Foulbriggis) between one and two miles outside the old walls of Edinburgh, and about three-quarters of a mile distant from the Castle on the Old Linlithgow road, which entered the capital by the West Port. Time, High-noon, 24th April, 1567.*

BOTHWELL (*enters from the right hand, followed by Captain* BLACKADDER, *both are in full armor. To those without*). Halt! Captain Blackadder send out patrols and make such dispositions, that no party from the West, many or few, upon the causeway, proper, on a by-road or across the fields, can reach the West Port without being intercepted. If a company should present itself in arms and make a show of fight, attack them instantly, but shoot no shot nor arrow. Do the work without noise and with cold steel. See to it; I trust to your experience and discretion. (*Exit* BLACKADDER L. H. *Drawing off his gauntlet and extricating a letter, which he reads.*) This is from my ladye-love. She tells me that until she lay at Linlithgow last night she had an escort of three hundred horsemen, but, there, got rid of them. My sweetheart is no fool and twists men round her fingers as deftly as she threads her needle.—Moreover, she bids me bring with me, a force full strong enough to crush out any opposition. I have anticipated both her fears and wishes, and a regiment more trustworthy in every respect, never followed a leader for a desperate adventure. (*Noise of a galloping a horse without,* L. H.)

PATROL (*without,* L. H.) Halt! Dismount! Whence? Whither?

FRENCH PARIS (*without*). A friend, from Linlithgow; dispatches for my Lord, the Earl of Bothwell.

PATROL (*without*). Pass, friend; but leave your horse.

Enter FRENCH PARIS, L. H.

BOTH. (*eagerly*). Well! Have you a letter; any token?

FRENCH P. Nothing; none is needed, mighty Lord. Everything is as you ordered. The Queen is even here, and has with her not to exceed a dozen riders.

BOTH. Any men of note?

FRENCH P. The Earl of Huntley, Sir William Maitland of Lethington, and Sir James Melvil. The rest are grooms and jackmen.

(*Renewed trampling of horses, without,* L. H.)

PATROL (*without,* L. H.) Halt!

CAPTAIN BLACKADDER (*without,* L. H.) Welcome, illustrious Princess!

MARY (*without*). What means this armed array? Where is the Earl of Bothwell?

BLACKADDER (*without*). A bow-shot distant by the bridge.

MARY (*without*). I will dismount; I am weary of the saddle; Huntley, Maitland and Melville follow me. Let the valetaille bide here.

MARY *enters* (L. H.), *accompanied by the* EARL OF HUNTLEY, LETHINGTON, MELVILLE, *and Captain* BLACKADDER *in the rear. These no sooner appear on the stage than a body of dismounted jackmen (spearmen) enter from both sides and form, so as to close every exit from the stage to any one.*

As MARY *advances* BOTHWELL *rushes to meet her, and kneeling kisses her hand. Before either can speak* MELVILLE *steps suddenly forward to separate them.*

MELVILLE. What means this violence?* Earl of Bothwell, does this mean ravishment? This is foul treason!

BOTH. (*with a sudden burst of fury*). False meddling fool, I'll stop your interference for all time, and send you to find out if that which your coadjutor Maitland doth deny exists; to Hell!

---

* Melville's sudden burst of loyalty is a very slight anachronism. It occurred elsewhere, but it did take place, and Mary barely saved her life.

(BOTHWELL *jerks out his dagger and strides furiously towards* MELVILLE. *The latter partially shelters himself behind* HUNTLEY, *while* MARY *throws herself between them.*)

MARY. Spare him, my Lord! For my sake, spare him. He is not worth your anger. He is no soldier, he is a mere courtier. He meant no harm; he merely asked what I now ask. Why do you meet me thus in arms and force?

BOTH. (*aside to.* MARY). Need we dissemble longer? (MARY *makes an affirmative sign.*) Captain Blackadder, look to these gentlemen. My Lords, Earls Huntley and Maitland; yes, Sir James, even you, you are in no danger for yourselves, but a mighty peril threatens her majesty in Edinburgh. This, I am here to prevent. She must away with me to Dunbar. Within its walls she is safe from every menace. With your permission, mighty Princess, we will set forth at once. (*Aside to* MARY.) Can you stand the journey. You know the road and distance well. (MARY *makes another affirmative sign, only visible to* BOTHWELL.) Captain Blackadder, get the men to horse; but sound no trumpet. We needs must arouse no question in the city. Send on ahead half a dozen of our best mounted troopers in order to have everything prepared and fitting for the reception of our sovereign lord, the Queen. Despatch! (*Exit* BLACKADDER, L. H. *An alarm bell rings out in Edinburgh.*) Hark! there is no time to lose! French Paris, conduct these gentlemen to their horses.

(*Exit* HUNTLEY, MELVILLE, LETHINGTON *and* FRENCH PARIS, L. H.)

BOTH. (*blows a whistle. Enter,* R. H., HAY OF TALLA). Laird of Talla, leave a strong rear-guard to cover and conceal our movements and keep back all pursuit. If possible, do not take life. (*A cannon shot, without, from the Castle of Edinburgh.*) Curses upon the fool; what means the Governor, Sir James Balfour. Can I trust that man? What means that shooting from the Castle. My Laird of Talla, we must not be pressed. You know your business. (*Another alarm bell rings.*) Ha! the Tocsin of St. Giles! (*Significantly.*) If necessary, kill! The Queen needs easy riding. We must not be pressed.

LAIRD OF TALLA. Make yourself easy; I know what you mean. I have made all my dispositions. (*Makes a military salute and exit,* R. H.)

Enter, L. H., CAPTAIN BLACKADDER.

BLACK. The advanced guard has marched. The Laird of Talla has some four hundred good sturdy men to hold the rear. The main body is composed of the pick of the whole force: they are in the saddle.

BOTH. (*to the Queen*). If you are ready, let us go.

MARY (*smiling, aside*). Ready, aye ready. (*She extends her hand to* BOTHWELL. *He takes it, kisses it and leads her forth,* L. H.)

BLACK. (*following*). I told that dry old quiz, Sir James Melville, that the Queen was ravished with her own consent. I rather think he'll find it so, and to his sorrow, when, once, he gets to Dunbar. (*Exit*, L. H.)

Between Scenes III. and IV., an interval of an afternoon and evening is supposed to elapse.

SCENE IV.—*An apartment in the Castle of Dunbar (destroyed within three years by the* EARL OF MURRAY, *after he had become Regent). Time, the night of 24th April, 1567; the same day* BOTHWELL *met Queen* MARY *at Fountain or Almond-Bridge, near Edinburgh, and had escorted her to the Fortress of Dunbar, of which he was Castellan.*

Ruins of Dunbar Castle.

BOTHWELL (*now in half armor, booted to the thigh, leads in* MARY, *still equipped for riding. He enters, speaking with severity, as if to others behind the scenes*). Look to yourselves, my Lords! We brook no interference. Blackadder, restore their swords and relieve them from guard and let them go. Although they are my foes and unfriends to the Queen, they need not fear if they comport themselves in peace and offer neither counsel nor resistance to my purposes. (*To* MARY.) This ends the farce and need of it. Why was it necessary that I thy lover should be put to this, and seem to seize at Fountain-Bridge, by force, what has been mine for years, my other self, my very self, my Mary?

MARY. 'Tis better so. This seeming justifies that upon which I have been long resolved. Although I have so often lain within thine arms—thy wife in all but the mere name—I yearned to be thy wife by right, all that I had been years, in soul, ay, a twelvemonth in very deed.

BOTH. It scarcely needed this; but still thy wish was law to thy true knight. When at that Annesley Supper eight earls—besides that subtle traitor, thy bastard brother, Murray, who had signed before—five bishops and eleven barons subscribed the Bond, pledging themselves, their sacred honor and their powers, to defend me against every calumny and charge of wrong doing, and avowing I was fittest mate for Scotland's queen, what need then of a seeming ravishment. When the wife, you made me wed, Jane Gordon, and her brother, earl and head of her house had, for a price—the Barony of Haddington and its dependencies—bargained, consented to a divorce; and Jane and I agreed that we should be put apart by every court has cognizance of such affairs in Scotland; it seems, to use the language of your creed, a work of supererogation to act the part of a foul ravishing. But still, my love, you willed it, and it is done.

MARY. Oh, Bothwell, little does your fearless heart understand my painful situation. Many, oh how many, flout your love for giving up her heart to thee, although acquitted by thy peers of all complicity in the murder of the wretched Darnley.

BOTH. (*interrupting her*). Murder! What term is this to me? Did I not act in strict accordance with your wishes, else had I done the deed openly, in the sight of day, yea, fearlessly, as I slew Elliott of the Park or would slay any one that came between thy heart and hand, thyself and me.

MARY (*laying her hand caressingly on his arm*). Bothwell, *my* James, between *us* this is comedy; but to the world a tragedy. Could I, by blood a Guise, be ignorant of the growing popular force and influence (*scornfully*)—out upon the hour that the people came to have a voice in the affairs of sovereigns! They must be conciliated with a show of deference to their opinions. We need but show a little deference—would I could better play the part—to blind them, lead them, rule them, as we will. This is but statescraft, policy, and conquers as surely as the slash of sword and crash of cannon. Now I am in thy power, in thy castle, helpless; a lone woman, in the grasp of one accused of conquering our sex by magic arts and philtres—nay, be not angry—fiercely as my soldier storms a breach.* Where do I now stand?

---

* While so very many pens—anxious to enlist in the romantic role of knight-errants—have devoted themselves in the endeavor to clear the character of Mary, invest her with more than mortal faculties, and even ascribe to her poetic genius, great powers at versification—which she did not possess—and assign to her the attributes of a real martyr—which she was not—since a true martyr must be, not only a victim, but an innocent one: every such romantic pen and pencil have ranged themselves with the

What foreign prince would seek the hand of Mary after the daring gallant, James Hepburn, had held her helpless over-night in his stronghold alone, without a chamber lady. (*Sadly.*) No sovereign prince; nay,

ranks of those devoted to the misrepresentation of her only true lover, her only constant and loyal champion, Bothwell. Michelet demonstrates how little truth can be placed in Brantome's testimony against him; and invalidates that, the only contemporary evidence, as to the want of manly beauty and grace in her life-long lover and third husband. Mary's statue in Westminster Abbey is as much a proof against her touching transcendant physical beauty as the only existing picture—the basis of all others—known as the Hardwick portrait.

She was not beautiful in the real sense of the word, but through other faculties as fascinating as a Circe, and Bothwell was, according to disinterested pen-portraits, an eminently attractive man. No authentic likeness of him exists, and—as is now almost universally admitted—he was a man renowned for qualities the most alluring to the opposite sex, and possessed of a loyalty beyond or equal to any proof and of a consummate courage, such as that with which even mythical heroes are seldom endowed. The fact is, he would rather kill than coax.

Even Gilbert Stuart—Mary's great partisan—drew a better picture of Bothwell, and gave him a higher character than the majority of historical writers prior to this generation; and Hosack, the Queen's Advocate, represents him as endowed with the noblest qualities a man can possess.

Stuart writes thus (160-2, 230-1, 237): "The breach between the Queen and her husband was already too great; and he [Murray] studied to make it irreparable. The Earl of Bothwell has acquired an ascendency in her councils; and he [Murray] courted him with assiduities and flattery. Mary herself was eager to bind them together in a lasting amity, and fancied to add to her happiness by the firmness of their union." * * *

James Hepburn, Earl of Bothwell, was born to an opulent fortune, and to an hereditary command over numerous retainers. *His fidelity to the crown had discovered itself during the struggles of the Reformation.* His zeal, services, and *sufferings* in that boisterous period, were distant recommendations of him. In the Rebellion excited by the Earl of Murray, his exertions were later and more interesting. But what chiefly *endeared* him to Mary, was the support he had afforded her against the murderers of David Rizzio. It was by his means, in a great measure, that she was enabled to recover her importance, and to chase them out of her kingdom. Her gratitude to him was excessive; and he improved the favorable impressions he had made, with unceasing *courtesy* and attention. By her favor he rose to *exercise all the power of government.* * * A boundless love of power, a fearless corruption, and a riotous prodigality were his characteristics. * * He could scheme the most criminal enterprises, and was desperate enough to put them in execution. * * *A polished exterior rendered his vices more dangerous.* HE WAS IN THE PRIME VIGOR OF LIFE; AND HIS PERSON AND BEHAVIOR WERE ATTRACTING. A passion for pleasure involved him in intrigues and gallantry. A taste for tri-*fles, elegance of address,* and *softness of manner, so alluring to women of every condition,* heightened the complaisance with which they naturally survey the imperfections of the voluptuous. ("*His merits, his address, his assiduity* and his persuasions overcame her." 230.) * * To establish himself in greatness, he was ready to perpetrate whatever is most flagitious, and could think without emotion of treachery, poison, and the dagger. The Earl of Murray, whom he wished to employ as a ladder to advance him to grandeur, penetrating into his character, availed himself of it; and he was utterly overthrown by a man, whose ambition was not less extravagant, but whose abilities, DISSIMULATION, and refinement, were far more transcendent and profound."

not a scion of a royal line would seek me for a mate, now that I have been thy spoil. (*Gaily*.) Nay, darling, if thy sweetheart marry must, she'd have to courtesy humbly for the hand of one of Scotland's rude and haughty lords—all whom I hate and loathe save thee, my love, my long-loved, trusted and faithful Hepburn. Yes, if I took a subject to my bed it could not be without the general feeling that what you rapt by force, by force you had enjoyed. Now, do you see into my little plot? The world knows not how long I have been thine in truth: thine every way. The game is now played out. We can afford to

---

"This fatal promise [to marry Bothwell], while it invigorated all his passions, gave a relief to the painful agitations of the Queen. The recentness of her terrors disposed her the more readily to give admittance to softer sensations; and he had too much gallantry not to press this advantage, and to display all the ardors of a lover. He even affected to have fears of the disappointment of his love. All her feelings were exquisite; and he knew how to awaken them. The elegance of their entertainment, of which he had previously been careful, their solitude and the near prospect of their indissoluble union, invited them to indulge in the delirium of pleasure. During twelve days she was under the dominion of *a young and agreeable*, a daring, and an unprincipled profligate; skillful in seduction and accustomed to impose on female frailty; *who could read in her look the emotions of her heart, and the secret workings of forbidden desires:* allure her mind to give itself up to the power of the imagination and the senses; take a pastime even in her pangs of remorse, and make them act as a zest to enjoyment; mark the conflicts and the progress of expiring virtue; and exult in the triumphs of sensibility over shame."

"After that Bothwell had anticipated with the Queen the tenderest rights of a husband, it was proper to think of the ceremonial of their marriage."

"It was only by slow degrees, and by habits of caution, vigilance, and address, that he could hope to be formidable. With the assistance of the Queen, it was his first care to uphold the splendor of the court; and, *immediately after the marriage, the Board of Privy Council reflected a heavy lustre to him by its distinction.* There assisted in it, the Earls of Huntley and Crawford, the Lords Fleming, Herries and Boyd, with the Archbishop of St. Andrews, and the Bishops of Galloway and Ross."

Crawford tell us Bothwell was "One of the handsomest men of his time;" "a man generally esteemed and applauded; the darling of the common people for his courage and liberality, and the envy of the court." Agnes Strickland admits, "As long as he [Bothwell] remained faithful to his duty, she [Mary] was safe." Proofs that Bothwell was the cynosure among his peers could be piled like Pelion upon Ossa." At quotation from Hosack must however close this note. "Bothwell was the only one of the great nobles of Scotland, who from first to last had remained faithful to her mother [Mary of Guise] and herself. * * Whatever may have been his follies or his crimes, *no man could say* JAMES HEPBURN *was either a hypocrite or a traitor. Though staunch to the religion he professed he never made it the cloak* of his ambition; though driven into exile and reduced to extreme poverty by the malice of his enemies *he never*, so far as we know, accepted of a foreign bribe. [Of what single other noble could this be said.] In an age when political fidelity was the rarest of virtues, we need not be surprised that his sovereign at this time trusted and rewarded him * * although the common people admired his liberality and courage ('his characteristic daring'). Bothwell among his brother nobles had no friends. Why? They envied his gifts and more his influence with the Queen. Need any man ask a higher eulogy than his enemies have been compelled to accord."

throw the cards away and grasp the stakes we have so subtly won. Who can gainsay our marriage now? The high nobility have urged me to wed thee as worthy my espousals. I agree. And now, like a knight errant, you have borne me off, as Pluto bore to Hades Proserpine. All that remains is but to wed, to wed before the world as we were wed when first I listened to thy passion's speech and gave myself in all, but name of wife, to thee. Carry me back to Edinburgh and there let holy church unite us by one rite, even though it be in secret. Then marry me in public by those forms to which you yield obedience —forms through which neither my love nor fond caresses, nay, my high commands could never make you break. Think you I do not honor you for that! The man that lives up to such motto of his house, "Klip Trest," and cannot be induced to swerve from that at the appeal of ambition, statescraft, nay, far more, of passion ; by the lure of the possession of the woman that he loves, that woman too a queen, a loving, lovely queen ; that is the man for me. Forgive that I have brought you to this pass ; and triumph with me that my Lorraine blood has loosed the knot and brought the end about; that Mary Stuart stands before the world so low in public estimation, and so high in her grand estimate of Bothwell, her own sore-tried lover, that she must wed him or sink so deep that she can never rise again. Do you imagine a woman can forget that which she bears within her bosom or the one beloved to whom it owes allegiance. Disannul the bonds that shackle thee before the world, never to me, and Mary will wed thee and glory in the doing it as woman never yet before did, or will do such deed. The tempest's passed, we have now reached our port, let us repair the past, and in each others arms forget what is foregone, and valiantly defy or trust the future. Take me—my king, my lover, husband, all in one—into thine arms, where I should have ever been, had I been ever bold towards thee as thou hast ever shown thyself valiant for me and mine. (*She throws herself into the arms of* BOTHWELL, *and then, after fondly caressing her, he leads her out.*)

An interval of about two weeks is supposed to elapse between Scenes IV. and V.)

SCENE V.—*Another Apartment in the Castle of Dunbar. Time, about the 1st May,* 1567. MARY *enters, followed by* BOTHWELL *reading a despatch.*

BOTHWELL (*striking, violently, the paper which he holds*). Dearest, I learn by this despatch, sent me by one in Edinburgh in whom I place implicit trust, that those same Lords, who, at the Annesley Supper, signed the bond urging you to wed with me and pledging "their lives, their fortunes and their honors" both to sustain and maintain us twain, are plotting now, again, against us both. Who could believe that men of such high standing could be guilty of such low practices—such infamy. The ink was scarcely dry upon the "Ainslie Supper Bond" when the principal lords who signed it entered, secretly, into another Bond to oppose the execution of the plan of what they had themselves suggested. They did not even wait for the consummation of the marriage, they had so hotly urged upon their Queen, before they bonded together to render the union void and negatory. They declare, false traitors as they are, that I desire and design to gain possession of the royal infant Prince in order to make way with him, even as I murdered his father,—a crime of which they themselves acquitted me and held me scathless, pledging all that men hold dear to uphold my innocence and support my dignity. By St. Bride of Bothwell, as Hereditary Lord High Admiral of Scotland, I have fought hard to clear its seas of the vilest scum of the ocean, the pirates that infested them, but what were they to these, the very scum, although high nobles, of the Earth. They make me revolt against my own humanity that I share the form and soul of such foul miscreants like them. Bothwell! Bothwell! you never stained your escutcheon with a lie, nor took a bribe, nor swerved from loyalty, nor played the hypocrite, nor used religion to cloak hypocrisy; how? how could you imagine that there could be such utter absence of all sense of honor from the souls of prelates and of peers? Out upon it! Fight, the last dread argument and resource of kings; they want it, eh? Well, they shall have it to the bitter end.

MARY. Unworthy and faithless traitors, as they styled themselves if they could or should prove false to these pledges. Infamous wretches; liars all, all the same ilk. They are all the tribe of Judas—beginning with that miserable Darnley. Is there any truth left on earth—at least in Scotland?

BOTH. It seems not. They charge that I have violated you here on the 25th of April,—by violence possessed myself of all long since was mine through infinite love and tenderness.

MARY. Why on that day, that very day, I came personally forward and issued a special authority to accomplish your divorce and set you free to wed me; yes, on that day, the suit of the Countess Jane was commenced before the Reformed Civil Court. When will these vilest accusations cease.

BOTH. I fear not till I grasp the truncheon of command, as sovereign and as consort, and set my iron heel upon the serpent's head and crush it. When that time comes, no more such ill-timed interference, sweetheart, as when you saved foul Lethington and fool Melville from my dagger's point. My love, your mercy is but weakness. For them, for men like Morton and your bastard brother, Murray, there is no safe recipes except that which Murray had for Huntley, Chastelard, John Gordon, and poor Davie—death!

MARY. I see it now; we will yet have the heads of one and all, from the Bastard down through the whole list of falsehood! Will we not, my Bothwell? I will not be merciful again, my own, unless you counsel it.

BOTH. And when I so advise, you need not fear to pardon. We must set forth for Edinburgh, there to be married and, to avoid all future questions, by *both* rites—in private by the forms that you respect; in public by the rites held sacred by me and by the majority of your subjects. You see the reason for all this: do you consent?

MARY. I do, my dearest James; your wishes are my own; your will my law; your thoughts my counsellors and guides; your will my judgment. Yes, our marriage must be hurried forward. The life I bear within me must not see the light to throw discredit on its authors: *that* allows no pause. So give your orders. Whatsoe'er they be I acquiesce in everything. I know that everything you do, is not only the wisest for you and me; my rights, our rights, and Scotland's weal.

BOTH. If the Fates smile upon us. *Fortuna sequatur:* if Fortune be propitious, love, we will crush out the whole brood of vipers. (*Blows a whistle. Enter* FRENCH PARIS.) Bid my adjutant, Captain Blackadder, summon to the field all who acknowledge fealty to the Hepburn and feel for Mary Stuart the full devotion that they owe their Queen. (*To* MARY.) Within ten days the Courts will set me free, and then our marriage must follow most incontinent.

FRENCH PARIS. Have you any further orders for your adjutant?

BOTH. Stay, follow me! It may be better to set down all things orderly in writing. The Queen and I will sign each document; she as the source of every power and grace, and I as her Lieutenant-General.

(*Exeunt* MARY *and* BOTHWELL, FRENCH PARIS *following.*)

Between Scenes V. and VI., an interval of several days is supposed to elapse.

Edinburgh Castle

SCENE VI.—*An open space in Edinburgh, in front of the Entrance and at the Foot of the ascent to the Castle. Time, 3d May, 1567. Groups of citizens and their wives crowd the front of the stage, engaged in animated conversation.*

A VOICE (*without*). Clear the way, they are close at hand.
MANY VOICES (*without*). God save the Queen!
(*Sound of approaching military music; drums and trumpets playing a march, rapidly approaching.*)
BOTHWELL (*without*). Cease playing! (*Music stops.*) My gallant men, throw down your lances. No faitour in Edinburgh shall have excuse to say that Bothwell brought back their sovereign liege, Queen Mary, with any show of force or aught of constraint upon her gracious will or person!
Enter MARY, *led by* BOTHWELL, *the latter richly but soberly attired in a dress trimmed with wild-cat fur. He is bareheaded, and carries his plumed bonnet in his hand. They are accompanied by the* EARL OF HUNTLEY *and suite,* CAPTAIN BLACKADDER, *Hackbutteers, Troopers dismounted, Attendants, &c. The Queen and* BOTHWELL *are preceded by trumpeters and drummers, and succeeded by soldiers and attendants. The military form in the rear of the stage and throw out guards toward the front, to keep back the crowd.*
MARY. Be covered, my dear lord; it ill befits the man who is to wed the Queen to stand uncovered in her presence. (*She playfully snatches his bonnet from his hand and places it on his head.*)
(*The populace stand silent.*)
CAPTAIN BLACKADDER (*to the crowd*). Why do you not cheer?

Have you no welcome for your Queen, and for the noble gentleman who is to wed her.

VOICES (*in the crowd*). We have no cheers for the murderer and murderess of Lord Darnley, our sweet King Henry, Lord Darnley.

BLACKADDER (*rushing into the crowd and striking several with the flat of his sword*). Out caitiffs, out! Cheer, or I will prick you with my sword's point until you cry out something.

(*A faint, quavering, unwilling cheer is given.*)

WOMAN'S VOICE (*in the crowd*). God bless your Majesty, if you had no art nor part in the slaying of the King, your husband.

Henry Stuart, Lord Darnley, King of Scots (murdered).
From an old print.

MARY. This is a sorry welcome for a sovereign to her capital. What a contrast to the welcome I received on my return from France, six years ago. And, yet, I was less happy then without you than now with you, my Bothwell!

Both. Thanks, my own sweet, for that kind word and thought. The weather welcomes us, if not these caitiff burghers, on whom the sun should frown. Auspicious be the omen that its brightness floods down on us advancing to our marriage. "Happy," says the proverb, "is the bride that the sun shines on" and oh, how lovely is this month of May!

Voice (*from the crowd*). "*Mense malas Maio nubere vulgus ait.*"
Woe! woe to those who marry in the month of May!

Mary. How ominous this cry!

Both. Nay, love; why pay a moment's heed to this rebellious crew. I will soon scourge them into submissive silence. (*Signs to* Captain Blackadder, *who goes out and returns with a body of Pikemen, who drive out the crowd, striking them over the head with the staves, and pricking them with the points of their lances.*)

Both. (*to the trumpeters*). Summon the Castle!

(*Flourish of trumpets. Enter from the rear* Sir James Balfour, *Deputy-Governor of Edinburgh Castle, with his Following, through the ranks of the soldiers in the background, which open to afford him passage. He pays obeisance to the Queen and* Bothwell *in dumb show.*)

Both. (*to* Mary). Give me your hand, my love! (*To* Sir James Balfour.) Show us the way, my own good Sir Deputy Provost. (*To* Captain Blackadder.) Marshal the troops, and forward.

(Captain Blackadder *motions the music to move off after* Sir James Balfour, *who passes through the Entrance Gate of the Castle, and then the troops, in the rear, face inwards and prepare to follow.*)

Both. Hold fast my hand, sweetheart. If we have none others with us but my brave Border Lairds and their bold followers, we have, in any event, each other. In, to the Castle! There we are masters of this rebel town. A few short hours and the rites of both our churches shall make us one in law—as we have long been one in heart—forever and forever!

(*As they turn to go, the trumpets and drums begin to sound a triumphal march; the Hackbutteers on the sides of the stage present arms, and then shoulder their muskets, the Troopers and Pikemen range themselves, and as the whole prepare to move, the crowd force themselves in again upon the stage wherever there is any space, and, amid martial music on the stage and a salvo of artillery from the Castle, without, the Curtain falls.*)

Borthwick Castle.

ACT V.

SCENE I.—*The beautiful and high-arched Great, or Banquetting, Hall of Borthwick Castle on the Gore.* Time, 7th of June, 1567; twenty-three days after the Marriage of* MARY *and* BOTHWELL.

Enter BOTHWELL *and* ORMISTON. *Both are in complete armor and carry their helmets in their hands.* BOTHWELL *strides to and fro, as if greatly exasperated.*

BOTHWELL. Damn this surprise! It is chargeable alone to the generalship of Kirkaldy of Grange. The others had neither hearts to dare nor brains to plan it. (*Reflectingly.*) When the Queen and I left Edinburgh, the sky seemed clear; horizon free of clouds, and, now, it is

---

* "BORTHWICK CASTLE. One and a half miles north of Crichton, equidistant between Tyne Head and Fushie Bridge Station, is the ruined *Castle of Borthwick*, a massive gloomy double tower, 90 feet high, 74 feet by 68 feet broad, and encompassed by a strongly fortified court, remarkable for the excellence of its masonry and the thickness of its walls. Built in the 15th century, in form it is nothing more than the old border keep, though on a larger scale than usual. The object of the Lord of Borthwick seems to have been to have all the space and accommodation of these cluster of edifices within the four (4) walls of his simple square block, and thus this building is believed to be the largest specimen of that class of architecture in Scotland."

"THE GREAT HALL is remarkable for some very fine carving, particularly over the

all clouded over with every sign of change ; impending tempest. Such is life—at all events, life in Scotland. (*To* ORMISTON.) Are you sure that we can trust our scouts, and the Castle is beset by not more than twelve hundred Border horsemen ?

ORMISTON. Perfectly sure, my Lord. They counted them when they first met under the Lords of Home and Morton. They had some seven hundred. Kirkaldy, Lindesay, assuredly, brought up not over five hundred more. This is some four or five days since. It is more likely that many of the moss-troopers have slunk off home, than that they have gained in numbers. Our scouts add, that many were unwilling to mount against your Earlship and the Queen ; but were enforced by threat of ban, outlawing, fire and halter.

BOTH. Have they any cannons ?
ORM. None.
BOTH. Many hackbutts ? (Muskets.)
ORM. The volleys that we hear show their supply of hand-cannon is most scant. Our scouts say few, and ill served at that. Home's troopers are poorly armed ; some few in steel and most in jacks. Morton's men are little better. Kirkaldy has a more trusty company.

BOTH. You are a staunch fellow, Ormiston, and fear neither man nor devil. These walls are strong and could laugh at cannon. If I leave a score of our best men, can you hold out a day or two against assault ?

---

fire-place, and a canopied niche in the side wall. Hither fled Queen Mary and Bothwell, 7th June, 1567, about a month after their marriage, on the alarm of the Confederate Lords gathering their forces against them. But they were scarce safe within the walls, when Lords Morton and Home, with a hostile array, appeared before them. Under these circumstances Bothwell first got clear away, and afterwards Mary (in the disguise of a page) to Dunbar. *One of the rooms is still traditionally called the* QUEEN's ROOM. In November, 1650, Cromwell, annoyed by a horde of moss-trooping marauders, who had taken post in Borthwick, sent a missive to Lord Borthwick, that if he did not "Walk away, and deliver his house," he would "bend his cannon against him," a threat which proved effectual, and prevented a bombardment. The parish church, which was rebuilt in 1865, is dedicated to St. Kentigern, and has an apsidal chancel. The manse of Borthwick was the birthplace of Robertson the historian.

"MURRAY's *Hand-book for Scotland.*"

"The castle of BOTHWELL's *friend*, LORD BORTHWICK, a baronial pile of magnificent aspect and vast strength, [is] situated in a lonely but fertile glen eleven miles south of the capital [Edinburgh]. On a rocky eminence, moated around by the waters of the Gore, the Donjon Tower of Borthwick, from its base to its projecting battlements, rises to the height of more than a hundred feet, with walls sixteen feet thick. A lofty barbican, flanked by a square and round embattled towers, slit by innumerable loopholes for arrows and musketry, together with a portcullis, double gates and draw-bridges, rendered it impregnable to the knights and horsemen of the Confederates, who were unprovided with artillery requisite for battering this stronghold, which is one of the finest examples of military architecture in Scotland ; and so grand and imposing is its aspect, that every visitor, on coming in sight of its gigantic facade, is impressed with silence and awe.   "GRANT's *Kirkaldy of Grange.*"

ORM. As long as victuals last, a scum like Home's would never dare assault.

BOTH. How many troopers have I in full armor, with strong long-winded horses?

ORM. Forty or fifty.

BOTH. Can I trust *you* to protect the Queen?

ORM. You can trust me to the death. Do I not fight with a halter round my neck? Did Morton, Home, or Lindesay catch me, I should have Jeddart justice—short shrift, however long the trial afterwards. (*Emphatically.*) My Lord of Bothwell, you know me.

BOTH. I do, old friend. I am resolved to sally forth, cut my way through, and raise the country. Within two days I will relieve you.

(*A volley of musketry fired without; one or two panes of glass are broken in the windows by the shots. Cries without,* Traitor! murderer! butcher! Come out and maintain the challenge you offered to those who charge you with the murder of the King! White livered hound, leave your leman! Come out and fight, if you dare!)

BOTHWELL (*without paying the slightest attention to the musketry, but roused by these words*). Ormiston, you hear this. I'll stand it no longer. Had it not been for the Queen, I would have cut my way out at the first. The man who spoke must be right near the castle. The clearness of the words prove that. Go pick out some good shot and shoot him dead! Get my men ready; bring out my horse! Be ready to throw open the gates, and drop the drawbridge! Go! you know your duty, go! (*To* ORMISTON, *about to leave.*) Stay! Dress a good tall youth in woman's garments. We'll have him in our midst, and the besetting force will think I am carrying off the Queen. If I get through, they'll think the Queen's escaped; and either rip their horses in pursuit or scatter and draw off when they believe the prize at which they aimed has 'scaped their clutches. Either way I shall succeed. Ormiston away; be quick! be quick!

(*As* ORMISTON *leaves the Hall, the* QUEEN *enters from the opposite side. She is dressed as a page, booted and spurred, and carries a riding whip in her hand.*)

BOTH. What means this dress, sweet one?

MARY. To ride forth with you. Have I not often said I wished I was a man to sleep in field, under the open sky, and be a trooper like my hero?

BOTH. (*embracing her*). Love, it would never do. Your pages jerkin would scarcely bide a shot, and poorest lance would run you through and through. (*Holding her at arms length and gazing at her with admiration.*) My own brave Mary, be patient! Trust Ormiston, and by

St. Bride of Bothwell within two days I will be back and blow off Home's and Morton's riff-raff like chaff.

(*Several musket-shots discharged overhead, and then a saker [small piece of artillery, 5¼ pdr. gun], followed by shouts of triumph within the Castle, and cries of dismay and horror without.* BOTHWELL *rushes towards the window to observe thence what has occurred.* MARY *restrains him.*)

MARY. My soul, my very life; be not so venturesome! At least put on your helmet. A stray shot might take the life which is my life.

ORM. (*runs in hastily, laughing*). My Lord, the men about us are the veriest cowards. The boasting blackguard, we heard just now a-railing, was hid in some tall gorse within long bow-shot, and in a hollow just beyond a dozen more lay hiding. We shot the fellow and, as the rest ran off, the saker killed another. (*Laughs immoderately.*) This startled the whole hive, and far and near you never saw such mounting and such flighting. They spurred and galloped as if they thought Mons-Meg was here from Edinburgh and going to open on them, and blow them over the Cheviots. Now, if ever, is the time to mount and sally.

BOTH. Let the men mount! (*Exit* ORMISTON.—BOTHWELL *presses* MARY *to his breast and kisses her passionately, then clasps on his helmet and rushes toward the door. As he reaches it he pauses.*) At midnight I shall be at the Black Castle, at Cakermuir. 'Tis only two miles distant. Fare thee well! (*Exit.*)

MARY. My own brave Bothwell! (*Looks after him with an eager passionate gaze.*) At the Black Castle! Cakermuir! I know the place.

(*Loud sound of the trampling of horses below. Then the clang of heavy gates thrown open violently, followed by the rattling of chains, and heavy fall of the drawbridge. Renewed trampling of horses, at first below, and then without. Shouts of* "A Bothwell! A Bothwell! St. Bride for Bothwell!" *The trampling of the horses and shouts recede. Distant musketry shots.*)

MARY (*rushes to the window and looks out*). My hero! not a man stands before him. They run like sheep chased by a wolf. Oh, that I were a man! Oh, that I were *such* a man! My own brave husband!
(*Scene closes before her.*)

Between Scenes I. *and* II. *nine or ten hours are supposed to elapse.*

SCENE II.—*The open Moor near the Black Castle, at Cakermuir. Time, towards daylight, 8th June,* 1567. BOTHWELL, *still in armor, is discovered whispering with* HAY OF TALLA. *Several troopers lie sleeping about with their lances piled. Another trooper, leaning on his lance, stands a sentinel at one side in the back-ground.*

BOTHWELL. How we scattered Home's and Morton's rabble. The coward scum! Thanks, brave Hay, for the stout troop you brought me. It is a darksome night. Can you make out a single light in Borthwick Castle?

HAY OF TALLA. No, not one. (*Enter* HEPBURN, *hastily*.)

HEPBURN. My Lord, I've seen a ghost, or else a spy, a minute or two since. Whether one or t'other it is all the same to Hepburn.

BOTH. A ghost! A spy! How? Where?

HEP. All of a sudden, looking towards Borthwick, a meteor flashed across the sky and by its glare, against a gorsey slope, I caught a glimpse of a horseman riding slowly, as if he had missed his way.

BOTH. How far away?

HEP. Perhaps a musket shot, not more.

BOTH. Off! Take half a dozen men and bring him in!

(*A horse neighs without, close at hand. A sentinel challenges without, followed by a Hurrah! And* MARY *enters, clad as in the preceding scene of this Act, followed by a group of astonished spearsmen.*)

BOTH. Gracious God! My wife! (*Throwing himself on his knee as* MARY *advances, catching her extended hand and covering it with kisses; then rising and clasping her in his arms.*) Blessed be St. Bride! Whence came you? How love, how?

MARY. After you galloped forth, my husband, the rebels seemed all in confusion. At first, from the battlements, we could see them riding off by scores and troops and hundreds, some in your track, some following other courses; until, at sunset, not a man could be discerned; and Bothwell and Ormiston sending forth some scouts, found all were gone. I wanted him to let me go forth, but he would not. He said that you had trusted him to guard me safe in Borthwick, until you relieved us. With you went forth my life. I could not stay cooped up there like a bird in a narrow cage, while you, my husband, was in the field. So I sat me down and wrote to Sir James Balfour of Pittendriech, your Deputy and Governor of Edinburgh Castle, ordering him to hold out stoutly for me; and to fire on the rebel Lords, if they attempted to quarter in the town. Vilest scum! no sooner were we married as they willed, than they began again to plot and plan and Bond against us. At the same time I wrote to the French Ambassador Du Croc, to see these Lords, and learn their real purposes. These orders I sent off by the young Laird of Reres. By this time it was night. When all was quiet I stole down from my chamber, gliding like a ghost into the banquetting hall, and by a cord let myself down from the window to the moat.

Borthwick Castle.

BOTH. My God! 'Tis some thirty feet: bravest of women! (*His armor rattling with his agitation.*) Whence was derived such courage, then ?

MARY. It seemed like nothing. Was I not flying to my Lord, my husband ? Did I not know where to find him ? Here!

BOTH. But where did you obtain a horse ?

MARY. 'Love laughs at locksmiths,' says the proverb, darling, and gold builds a bridge across the widest stream. Two of my women helped to lower me from the window. As expected, the postern stood unlocked by that same golden key. Then I scrambled through the moat, and up the grassy counterscarp, on, into the open ground. Thus, my Bothwell, I found myself beyond the ditch and there, close by it, a close-cropped nag, bridled and saddled, held by a faithful groom of low degree. We'll raise him up, my Bothwell, and fill his pouch with Mary Reals (or Cruickston Dollars). I knew the country well, and while the light lasted, marked well the direction of the Black Castle you had mentioned as you parted. Crichton Muir was no strange place to me.

Have I not galloped over it, hawking, with you beside me, husband, when I but little dreamed we ever should be man and wife.

BOTH. But the night has been very dark.

MARY. Husband, you forget the glowworms; the Muir is famous for them at this season. The gorse was all aflame with those stars of the green earth!

BOTH. Bravest of women, and you encountered no one?

MARY. Not a shadow crossed my path, and if aught did (*laughing merrily*), did I not have my sword, and have I not ridden like a trooper with pistols in my holsters, and am I not Bothwell's love and wife, and (*drawing herself up proudly*) am I not Mary Stuart, Queen of Scotland?

BOTH. God's blessing upon thee, best and bravest woman! (*Clasps her in his arms.*) And now to horse, we must breakfast in Dunbar. (*To* HEPBURN.) There is no longer need of secrecy. Have I not here my dearest and my Queen? The country is alive with friends. Lords Seton, Yestor and Borthwick, together with the Lairds of Walkton, Bass, Black Ormiston of that Ilk, and he of Lothian, Wedderburn, Blackadder and Laughton, are all in saddle, gathering to my standard. The Border Bonnet Lairds, with every man that they can raise are spurring to Dunbar. Morton and Home with their whole rebel force following, have ridden fast as nags can carry them to Edinburgh. Sound trumpet! Sound to horse! Blow merrily! To horse! To horse! To horse! On to Dunbar!

Ruins of Dunbar Castle.

(*Trumpet sounds "Boots and Saddles." The call is repeated from point to point without. Finally the different trumpeters unite in a triumphant Fanfare, amid which the scene closes in front of them.*)

Six days are supposed to elapse between Scenes II. and III.

SCENE III.—LETHINGTON's *chambers in Edinburgh.* LETHINGTON *enters reading a despatch;* MORTON *meeting, interrupts him.*

MORTON. Maitland, you do not believe in God! You must perforce believe in the devil; for never was a plot concocted with human cunning and wickedness, such as ours, that could have succeeded without the help of Auld Hornie himself. Do you remember our first

(From an old engraving.)

conference in my chambers, shortly after Mary Stuart's marriage? To complete the split between the Queen and Darnley, we had to bring the silly long laddie to believe in Rizzio's intimacy with his wife. The Italian was disposed of. He troubled us no more.

LETHINGTON. True! That was sagaciously accomplished and converted the Queen's disgust for her faithless, brutal, cowardly consort, into that positive hatred that sprung the mine at Kirk-o'-Field.

MOR. (*with a subdued laugh*). How the dolt walked into the toils! No silly rabbit was ever toled by a turnip into a trap more easily (*Laughs.*) Darnley traveled to his death as complacently as a cosset lamb is led in to the shambles.

LETH. Who could have believed that "Gloriosus" Bothwell could be brought to serve our purposes so perfectly. And, yet, it is not so wonderful. Loyal, himself, he cannot see into the depths of our disloyalty to everything but our own interests. We understand each other. He comprehends nothing beyond his love for Mary and his hopes for Scotland. He seeks to rule the realm, not for his own advantage, but for the welfare of the people, the glory of the Queen, and his own credit—without a party too, by his own bravery; the honest fool! Countries are not ruled so—men cannot rule except through parties, partisans and passion. His affection for the Queen was of such sterling stuff, that it even stood the test of her injustice, and her sudden, unrestrained longing for a far lesser man. Think you, he would have stood the arrogance of Murray had he not loved the Queen in spite of every wrong?

MOR. Justly are you styled the Chameleon. You change with every phase of circumstance. Were you not caught by Mary?

LETH. (*drawing himself up*). That is my own concern, Earl Morton. Let alone my personal affairs! Let us resume our business. Darnley dead, Bothwell acquitted and married to the Queen, our pear is ripe, and ready to drop into our hands. This requires but a breath of popular opinion. How I scorn the popular thought and voice! Popular opinion, forsooth; the first so easily misled, the second roused to fury by such little cause or without right. "The 'generous people' (*sarcastically*), so much more capable of what may be called the poetry of sentiment than of true feeling." Through it we are masters of the capital. The vast majority believe that Bothwell seeks possession of the Royal infant, Mary's child by Darnley, or perhaps by Davie—who knows that—to rid himself of him as he and we rid both of the child's father. Now, away with him! Away with Mary! Murray becomes Regent. He, again, is but a tool; and all Scotland from the Clyde unto the Shetlands is ours, ours, all ours!

MOR. And, yet, it seems that we must fight for it, and that God which you deny has shown himself throughout all time, The Lord of Hosts and God of Battles.

LETH. Tush, Morton! With all your worldly sense and knowledge of mankind, you cannot get rid of the old religious leaven, the seed sown at your mother's knee and fostered by John Knox. Did not John Knox advise the death of Rizzio, connive at murder, thunder from the pulpit against the Papist Darnley and the Pope's agent Rizzio? Priest and minister, they are alike, and selfish interest is the hand that guides. The Queen is fickle. With legal right and sole possession will come satiety. I know her thoroughly. Her passion sated for the nonce, she must be made to separate from Bothwell and trust in us.

Mor. This seems past hope! We thought we had her when she and he were caught in Borthwick Castle; and yet he cut his way out like a brave fellow as he is, and she, apparelled as a trooper, booted and spurred, straddling her saddle like a man, stole forth and joined her lover-husband, fled to him as when he lay wounded at the Hermitage, as the old song runs—

"Some mair about the Queene is saed,
And how ye Earle got wounded :
How she, towards him, to see him fledde—
The which she very soon did."

Hermitage Castle.

Leth. Love thrives on opposition in a wayward, imperious woman. Kirkaldy, with all his boasted chivalry, is playing around the bait of this Scotch siren. We must so pitch the hook that it catches in his gills. The Queen believes that he is honest; that if she but accepts him as a pilot for the time, and furls her sails, she can bid defiance to the squall, and with serener weather take Bothwell to her arms again, as captain, and sail on with him in peace. (*Trumpet without.*) She was grievously mistaken in Darnley, but she errs more fatally in her judgment of Kirkaldy. We must keep in with him, for now he looms up as our decoy to win her confidence from Bothwell, as the farmer's use a tulchan-calf to induce a cow which has lost her young to let down her milk. With all his gilt of chivalry, Kirkaldy has his price, and can play knight or knave, patriot or informer, good friend or spy, as the wind sets and his purpose jumps. John Knox knew his real nature. Kirkaldy, if not a murderer in fact, is a murderer at heart, as cold-blooded as any of the worst of our party. But— hark ! (*A trumpet sounds without.*)

Mor. That does not sound like peace. (*Opening the window and leaning out*). Ho, sir! What are the news ?

Voice (*without*). The army of the Queen is marching upon Edinburgh. Our scouts have brought the news that their light-horse have been already discovered from the platform of the Castle.

Mor. (*to the speaker, without*). Thanks, friend! (*Shutting the window and turning to* Lethington.) This looks very much like a fight, and the chances are not in our favor, certainly not the right. (*Sarcastically*.) Remember the Round-about-Raid !

Leth.* One of the wise captains of antiquity, on being told that the enemy were advancing and were determined to fight, replied, "That will be just as we may choose." The man was a great general. We must show wise leaders still are living. There will be no fight, Earl Morton ; you play at whist ! Who understands the game and holds the leading trumps and strongest cards must win, unless he throws his luck away. Kirkaldy is the winning trump this time, and I can play him. We must take the saddle. Be calm and trust in me ! I tell you, Kirkaldy is our winning card, and he is in my hand. (*Exit.*)

Morton (*lingers in deep thought. Cannon shot without*). Ha ! What does that mean ? Can it be Balfour, from the castle, firing on the city !
Off, Morton, off! Matters brook no delay :
Bothwell or I must conquer Scotland's sway !

Scene closes as near as possible to the front, so as to afford space and opportunity to arrange Scene IV. behind it.

Forty-eight hours are supposed to elapse between Scenes III. and IV.

---

* No likeness of this Maitland (the younger) of Lethington could be obtained for this play which was sharp enough to be reproduced by photo-engraving for printing. No portrait of Kirkaldy of Grange is known to exist.

Mary Stuart, Queen of Scots.
From the famous portrait in the gallery of the Hermitage Palace, St. Petersburgh, Russia.
Originally in Paris, France, prior to the great French Revolution.

Demi-Lancer, Trooper in puffed and ribbed armor and Yeoman of the Guard.
Middle of the XVI. Century.

SCENE IV.—*Carberry Hill.** Time, Afternoon of 15th June, 1567. A knoll, whence the prospect extends to the westward and northward, looking over the nearer lines of the Queen's forces, and toward those, beyond, of the Confederate Lords. In the immediate rear*

---

* The Confederates [Rebels] marched eastward against [Dunbar], from which Mary had issued her proclamation for mustering an army in defence of her person. It was not obeyed save by Bothwell's immediate allies, by whose exertions the Queen soon beheld four thousand brave men of Lothian and the Merse arrayed under her standard. Bothwell had a guard, or chosen band, of two hundred [hackbutteers or] harquebussiers and the royal stores at Dunbar furnished his troops with falcons, or light [6 pdr.] field-pieces. While her forces were rapidly increasing, the Queen marched to Gladsmuir, and occupied the lofty tower of Seatoun; her soldiers were meantime cantoned in the adjacent villages of Preston, Tranent and Cockenzie. After halting for a night at Musselburg, the Confederates, as they marched out of that ancient and picturesque little town, with trumpets sounding and kettle-drums beating, amid the clamor of the inhabitants and the tolling of bells, learned that the forces of Mary, led by the Duke of Orkney, were in position on the HILL OF CARBERRY, an eminence above the town, commanding an extensive prospect of the sea and surrounding country. On the summit of that hill, now known as the QUEEN'S SEAT, Mary held with Sir William Kirkaldy that conference which was to have so much influence on her future destiny. It is now covered with the richest copsewood: *then it was bleak and bare*, or studded

stand three pieces of artillery (falcons or 6 pdrs.), pointed at the latter, with a few "Constables" in charge: of whom one, assigned to each gun, at intervals waves his linstock to keep the slow-match alight and ready for immediate use. Near these are groups of

only by the tufts of dark evergreen whin [furze, gorse] or the golden bells of the yellow broom ; and *a rough block of stone on its summit formed a seat for the unfortunate* MARY.

It was the morning of Sunday the 15th of June [1567] ; the weather was intensely hot, and the troops of both factions suffered considerable annoyance from the clouds of dust, the closeness of the atmosphere, and the burning rays of the unclouded sun, which darted on their *shining armor*. Bothwell—or the Duke of Orkney—commanded the whole of Mary's little force, having under him the Lords Seatoun, Yester and Borthwick, with four Barons of the Merse—viz., Wedderburn, Langton, Cumledge and Hirsel ; and those of the Bass, Waughton, Ormiston in Lothian, and Ormiston of that Ilk, in Teviotdale, all men of courage and high descent.

The Confederates were formed in two columns : Alexander, Lord Home and the Earl of Morton led the first, and Athol the second, with Glencairn, Ruthven, Semphill and Sanquhar. Kirkaldy, with his two hundred spears, had galloped eastward, to get in between Bothwell and the Castle of Dunbar, hoping to cut off his retreat, and by a sudden charge break the array of his cannoneers.

The main body of the Confederates were drawn up with their left flank to the sea, almost on the same ground which, twenty years before, had witnessed the unfortunate Battle of Pinkie. On both sides the numbers were now nearly equal, but they differed greatly in discipline.

The army of Mary consisted of a hastily-mustered and inexperienced multitude, while that of the Confederates was principally composed of gentlemen [perjured villians of high birth, renowned for courage, and brave as they were determined].

The ground where those adverse bands drew up for battle is now covered with groves of the most luxuriant wood and studded with modern villas. In those days it exhibited but two solitary shepherds' huts and Pinkie Burn winding between banks of willows, sedges and reeds ; the old taper spire of St. Michael's Kirk, an edifice of unknown antiquity, built of stone squared by Roman hands, rose on the Mount of the Prætorium above the wooded banks of the Esk ; which, after making a beautiful sweep around it, and passing under the steep old Roman bridge of three arches, which, a thousand years before, had connected the Castrum with the Municipium, flows into the Forth between Fisherrow and Musselburgh. The latter was then, as now, a straggling and irregular burgh, with gable-ended streets, by the ruined chapel of Lorretto, and the tall old manor-house of Pinkie, with its picturesque turrets overtopping its dark and shadowy groves. It was then the residence of Kirkaldy's foeman, Durie of that Ilk, Abbot of Dunfermline, who, prior to the Reformation, had been Lord Superior of Musselburgh. Such was the prospect from the hill—

"Where Mary agonizéd stood,
And saw contending hosts below
Press forward to the deadly feud,
With hilt to hilt, and hand to hand,
The children of our mother land
For battle met ! The banners flaunted
Amid Carberry's beechen grove ;
And kinsmen braving kinsmen strove
Undaunting and undaunted."—

royal, regular Hackbutteers, belonging to the Queen's body-guard, at ease, and parties of Border noblemen and their retainers, Jackmen, evidently as if just dismounted, and leaning on their long spears. In the front centre are MARY STUART *and* BOTHWELL; *and, to the right, but withdrawn a space,* KIRKALDY OF GRANGE. *Behind the Queen is* CAPTAIN BLACKADDER, *one of* BOTHWELL'S *subordinates, watching what is occurring in the enemy's ranks and his remarks serve as an explanation or* CHORUS.

BLACKADDER (*to* BOTHWELL). Hasten, my Lord, your colloquy: the foe
    Are striving to outflank us. Look, their horse
    To close the road to Dunbar, headlong spur.
    If fight 's the word, now is the time to fight,
    Lest we both lose advantage of the sun
    Full in their faces; our position too;
    And worst, if beaten, our retreat 's cut off.
(*Finding* BOTHWELL *does not pay immediate attention, raising his voice.*)
    Mighty earl, great Captain! Here we stand not
    To hear the nightingale's sweet am'rous notes,
    But hearken to the trumpet's points of war—
    Then bid them sound! Shoot falcons and set on!

An ancient trench, which had been formed by the English in 1547, lay before the line of Mary's forces; and on the summit of this Bothwell, gallantly arrayed in brilliant armor, "showed himself, mounted on a brave steed." *He was well known to be an accomplished knight and fearless horseman.* * * If anything could have retrieved her affairs at this desperate crisis, it must have been a headlong advance under cover of a cannonade; and Bothwell should have instantly led on the soldiers of Mary to victory or death; instead of which, while anxiously awaiting the arrival of Lord Herries and others with reinforcements, he suffered an ineffectual negotiation to take place by means of the French ambassador. * * *

"We came not to this field," sternly added Alexander, Earl of Glencairn, "to ask pardon for what we have done, but to yield it unto those who have offended!" Du Crocq, finding it vain to expect an accommodation with such intractable spirits, bade adieu to the queen, and with his train departed for Edinburgh.

Alive to the perils of her situation, the unhappy Queen saw fully the manifold dangers which environed her. * * On her palfry she rode through the ranks of her little host, but found the soldiers dispirited, fatigued and viewing her coldly. Many, who were overcome by the heat of the weather, stole from their places to quench their thirst in Pinkie Burn, but forgot to rejoin their colors; others deserted openly in bands, and none appeared to remain staunch to her but Bothwell's band of Harquebussiers, and the immediate vassals of the House of Hepburn. It was at this crisis that Kirkaldy's squadron, after encompassing the hill, halted; when Bothwell, perceiving his flank turned, and matters becoming desperate, sent down a herald-at-arms with a gauntlet of defiance, offering by a single combat to prove his innocence of King Henry's murder.   GRANT'S "*Kirkaldy of Grange.*"

MARY (*continuing a conversation which had been going on before the scene opened*). I am resolved to trust Kirkaldy—
BOTHWELL.   Ah!
What glamour blinds thee, love? Thou know'st him not:
The hireling spy and England's trait'rous tool.
He but deceives thee, with his specious tale;
His boasted chivalry 'tis mere lacker.
Beneath the semblance of the golden truth
Is falsehood's foul and cheap-jack metal. Think
Ere you commit your fortune to such crew.

Archers. Pikemen, Border-troopers and Arquebussiers or Hackbutteers (Musketeers). Middle of the XVI. Century.

(BOTHWELL *breaks off suddenly, rushes to a Hackbutteer, and, by signs and words inaudible to the spectators, directs him to shoot Kirkaldy, who, shading his eyes against the declining sun, is looking in a different direction towards his own friends.* MARY, *moved by* BOTHWELL'S *charges, seems lost for a moment in deep thought; then suddenly perceives* BOTHWELL'S *intention and throws herself between the musketeer and his aim.*)

MARY. What would'st thou do?
BOTH.   Slay the deceiving villain
Who has infatuated you.

BLACKADDER (*plucking at* BOTHWELL'S *gauntlet and striving to attract the Earl's attention and addressing him, half-aside*). She's fey!
That is the the truest word you ever spoke:
My Lord! I've heard of bogles, and such like de'ils
Which borrow women's forms to ruin men—
I've followed you, thro' thick and thin, my Lord!
With dog's unquestioning fidelity;
Wages but little save the fame and game—
Which I discern that we have played and lost.
This Queen, for whom you've ventur'd life and soul,
Honors and lands, all thou hast heir'd and won,
This Mary Stuart is just such a de'il
As I have heard describ'd by Master Knox.
She's taken with a sudden frenzy for this Grange,
And like a thunderstorm, that's fierce but short,
Will damage do as big as autumn storm.
She's kindled him with lightning of her eyes,
And his responsive, flaming, flash to hers
With what belongs to you and no one else.
Think but of yourself, my Lord! Let's away
Whilst chance there is, this most mischanceful day.
MARY (*discerning that* BOTHWELL *is making up his mind to attack* KIRKALDY.)
He's under safeguard of my queenly word,
And, though he were the very knave thou say'st,
He must not die by an assassin shot.
BOTH. (*with difficulty restraining himself, and making a gesture to the musketeer to "recover arms," returns to the Queen's side*).
My love, my food, my sweetheart and my life,
Thy noble nature and thy native sense
Are both the victims of this knave's device.
Is it not better, here upon this field,
To strike one blow for honor and thy crown
Than thus abase thyself to traitors—yield
Thy freedom, and perchance thy life, to those
Who never yet have kept a single Bond
Beyond the signing, had their purposes
But borne their fruit perfidious. Hast thou not
Prov'd me, as woman never yet prov'd man
Or had the chance to do 't? Have I not shown,
By ev'ry thought, word, act, since manhood's dawn,
That Truth and Bothwell were synonymous?
"Kiip Trest!" my motto—emblem of mine life.

Was I not faithful to thy mother; then
With equal truth did I not turn to thee:
Until thy love, enkindled at my own,
Or my big love, inflam'd by thy bright eyes,
Converted me from loyalty to love?
Have I e'er fail'd thee? Have I not been truth,
Love, faith, devotion: *all* thy sex can ask?
And yet thou dost not trust me; but prefer'st
The specious promise of a hireling tongue?
MARY. I am resolved to trust the Bonded Lords;
Not, that I have lost faith in thee, my own,
But 'cause 't would seem as if by Fate impell'd,
This is the wisest course and fits the time.
Look but around! Fighting is madness now.
Our army's gone to water save some few
Brave Border Jackmen and the Hackbutteers:
Besides some sixty Lairds and henchmen true,
The Constables, and our own following—
Our body guard, some cannoneers and spears—
The whole array's disbanded. There's nothing left!
My own dear life, so that I *can* save you
All's sav'd, I hold's worth saving, here, on earth.
Do you believe that with the life you've given,
Pulsating in my bosom, I could say
Leave me an hour, did I not firmly think
That a short space would bring you back again:
Did I not *so* believe, I swear, my James!
I would far rather perish here, at once,
In very desperation, than say, Go!
A brief, sad parting and a better meeting
May bring again a long and halcyon term.
BOTH. No, no! No, no! I tell thee, No! 'T would seem
As if, on board a stout, still lusty, frigate,
Because 't is slightly shatter'd by a squall,
Thou would'st abandon ship and practic'd captain,
To trust a pirate's skiff to save from storm
That lowers, but has not burst. Oh! Mary,
Dost thou love me?
MARY.   My acts are the best answer.
I have gone through too much for thee to doubt it.
Oh, what have I not done to prove my love?
Oh, what have I not suffer'd to be thine? (*Wringing her hands.*)
BOTH. Then, by the tie united us when twain,

      And by the two church rites that made us one,
      I do conjure thee, let me fight this day:
      Not like a felon bid me steal away.
      Never before has Bothwell quit the field,
      But all victorious or upon his shield.

(BOTHWELL *takes* MARY's *hand in his, and they stand thus, grasping each others hands, for some minutes; then clasp each other in a sad but fierce embrace. He glues his lips to hers, then suddenly releases her and, gazing, seems to discern that neither kisses nor caresses have changed her resolution. His eyes question her.*)

MARY (*suddenly*). I am resolv'd to keep my word to Grange.
BOTH. Oh, love! my life!
MARY (*with a sad smile.*) Alas! we here must part;
      Part for a time, assur'd of future meeting.
BOTH. Wilt thou be true to me and keep thy promise,
      So often sealed with kisses, e'en beside
      The dead man's corse; to ne'er even in thought,
      Nor word, nor bond, nor deed, annul nor weaken it;
      Be my own Mary, till the whelming sea
      Or the cold earth put seal to either life?
MARY. I promise. Go! Before it is too late,
      Take horse for Dunbar, ere the foemen's horse
      Out in and make escape impossible.
BOTH. Oh, woman! Woman, what art thou but guile?
      'Tis as I feared; the woman is bewitch'd.
      No sooner were we married than I saw
      That she resisted—as a restive horse
      Rebels against the curb—against the tie
      That made her wife and leash'd her to a mate.
      Alas! alas! a sudden, frenzied spasm
      Sets her on fire with passion for this knight;
      An overmast'ring passion. Was I wrong
      To be so jealous, and to guard myself
      Against a change; dishonor to my bed?
      Let the world talk, my duty I have done
      And all is lost that I, so hardly, won.
      Still midst thy weakness Bothwell will be strong,
      My brilliant constancy shall luminate
      The blackness of thy mind's eclipse;
      Yes, light our future if the Fates permit.
      I lov'd thee queen and woman, as a man
      And knight should love. Fate must the Problem solve;

This I do feel whatever ill befalls us
All who conspir'd to our separation
Will perish in their prime, ay, even when
Their fingers grasp the prize for which they sold
Their lives, their souls, their honors. Now, farewell!
My heart is thine forever. With Bothwell,
Arm'd at thy side, thou wer't a queen supreme.
Betrayer and betrayed; be false to me
And set thy fame and fortune both alike.
Calvin was right, who said, "who damn'd will be,
Will be!" Fair woman, whom, accosted, straight
I won; I saw you, and you conquer'd me:
As a slave led me, as Cleopatra
Led Antony: and now when all our future
Hangs on decision, you, the boldest, blench
And yield. Strike but one blow for victory!
For God's sake, Love's sake, let me strike one blow.
(*Pauses for a reply, then, with desperation.*)
Will you not fight, or let us fight?

MARY. Too late! *

---

* Almost every writer who has written upon this epoch, as well as readers of the narratives of these events, have concluded that, because there was neither manœuvering nor fighting at Carberry Hill, Bothwell displayed no ability as a commander nor manhood as an individual. The French ambassador's testimony is sufficient to prove his aptness as a general, and Mary forbade any action which could demonstrate that he was not a thorough soldier.

The absolute contrary of the general calumny is the truth. All that a captain and warrior could do he did, and endeavored to do. Mary was the sole cause of his and her disasters. She insisted on hurrying to meet her enemies, when the simple delay of a few days would have ruined them; and then, when audacious-promptness was the requisite of the moment and would have condoned the previous error of mistaken impulse, she wavered, and let the chance go by. Mary has been almost invariably credited with good sense. She did not possess it; smartness she did. Whenever she undertook grand or efficient measures she fell below the occasion and manifested no sense. At Langside—as frequently referred to—her defeat was due as much to her own decision and indecision as to the selfish intentions and evil counsels of others.

As everywhere else, when called upon to display combined courage and discretion, she betrayed herself. As it was in her operations against Huntley, in 1562, so it was on Sunday, 15th June, 1567; so it was in her resolution to take refuge in England. When she permitted Bothwell to have his own way, as she did during the " Run-about-raid " and after Rizzio's murder, all went admirably, and she was triumphant whenever Bothwell's counsels were implicitly followed. The "Great Earl's" Russo-German champion, Petrick, justly observes, "The facts are manifoldly [and manifestly] distorted; they envelop Bothwell, like the opaque mists evoked by a magician, and in them this important personage again sinks into deep obscurity."

At Carberry Hill, she alone betrayed herself, her husband, and the friends of both. At Langside, she again both betrayed herself and was betrayed. Stevenson and Nau express this: "During the Queen's stay at Hamilton many difficulties arose among the lords and the other leading men of her court. In the opinion of many it was

(BOTHWELL *seizes her in his arms and kisses her wildly; but, seeing that even in this supreme moment she makes a motion for* KIRKALDY *to approach, he suddenly releases her and strides to the left of the stage; then turns, and perceives that* KIRKALDY *has drawn nearer to the Queen. Some one in the rear has given a signal to the enemy, and without, to the right, arise shouts, fanfares of trumpets and triumphant flams of drums.*)

BOTH. (*with concentrated bitterness*). *Varium et mutabile semper Fœmina!* Thus sang the Mantuan Bard.
With truth outlives the bush that furnished bays.
And for this fickle creature I have lost
Country and honor—all a man holds dear.
Oh! cruel Fortune. I have lov'd, have lost!
All! all is lost! I am a wretch indeed.

(*Wrings his gauntletted hands, then lets them fall disconsolately. Suddenly rousing himself, and speaking to those without.*)
Ho! To horse! To horse!

Arms and Armor. Middle of the XVI. Century.

---

inexpedient that she should remain in the hands of the Hamiltons. *Not only was the personal safety of her majesty compromised hereby, but further, many persons who*

MARY (*giving her hand to* KIRKALDY). Come, Sir, let us go!

(*These two last exclamations are simultaneous as the curtain falls. Rude, loud, triumphant music accompanies its descent, which gradually changes into softer and mournful notes, as the curtain again rises upon a double scene.*)

FOTHERINGAY.	DRAGSHOLM.
Mary, with her head on the block, the executioner standing over her with uplifted axe.	Bothwell lying dead upon the floor of his prison in Adelsborg Castle,* Denmark.

Curtain falls again to sad music, which gradually changes into a Symphony, as it rises on the reunion of MARY *and* BOTHWELL *in another sphere.*

---

were at enmity with that house refused to join her." [Burton (IV. 372.) adds, "The Hamiltons have been blamed in recommending it [the march which involved a battle] with *a treacherous purpose.*"] " Hereupon it was decided that she should retire to Dumbarton, where every one could have free access to her." Langside interposed !

* " We may add," Lord Mahon goes on to say, " we have doubts whether Bothwell's confinement in Denmark was so strict and rigorous as most histories allege. Such a statement appears scarcely compatible with the following expressions of a letter from Queen Elizabeth to the King of Denmark, in 1570."—(*Translation from the Latin.*) " Concering Bothwell, we have certainly written at previous dates to your Serene Highness, as the undoubted murderer of his King. [Here, Elizabeth, in her thirst for Bothwell's blood, accords the title of King to Darnley, which she consistently denied to him while alive.] * * * wherefore, to sum up, we trust (which, nevertheless, we have besought of your Serene Highness again and again), that the associate in a deed of turpitude, may be confined in a dungeon and in chains in one of your state-prisons, or certainly, as we would prefer and rather beg that he should be taken from his dungeon to uudergo trial for his crime in that place (before such tribunal), whither such admitted wickedness should be transferred, for neither, assuredly, is it honorable for the King [Frederick] that the murderer of a King [Darnley] should be permitted to move about freely, without restraint (or genteely), and live without any punishment."

Kirkaldy of Grange.

"That a career so honorable [as that of Kirkaldy of Grange] should have closed in shame and disgrace is one of those anomalies in human history of which it is rarely possible to offer any adequate explanation. When the hope of the defeated [Queen's] party had become desperate; when Elizabeth had shown publicly her determination that the Catholics should never triumph in Scotland; when everything which he most desired had been obtained, and what he most hated was lying prostrate and disarmed, suddenly,—with what motive who can tell,—he changed sides, became the champion of the Queen, whom he had assisted to dethrone; the enemy of the Kirk, of which he still continued a professed member: and after having filled Scotland for four years with a horrible war in a desperate cause; after involving himself in miserable intrigues with the French and the Spaniards to destroy Elizabeth, and make Mary Stuart Queen of England—that very Mary Stuart *whose fiercest accuser he himself had been, and whom he never, even after he had become her champion, professed to acquit of the crimes with which he had charged her*—he closed this shameful palinodia [recantation] of a once honorable life where alone, as now we see it, it was possible for such a course to end—on the gallows. No one will call in question the justice of his end who is acquainted with the detail of the war for which he was responsible; but of the motives which could have induced him to follow a course so unlike himself, so inherently disgraceful, and so desperate in its chances of success, no historian that we know of has offered so much as an attempt at explanation."—*Fraser's Magazine*, Vol. 47, p. 535.

Bothwell's Advantages.

Teulet, in his Preface, xxi., says that, besides the Casket Letters, a multitude of contemporaneous documents prove the violent, boundless passion of Mary for Bothwell, who possessed all the physical advantages proper to seduce a young woman, and was only a few years older than the Queen; since, when they were married, in 1567 (15th May), he was about thirty, and Mary (born 5th December, 1542) was twenty-five years and five months old.

ERRATA.

Page 27, 28. "Guistizia," should read: Giustizia.
" 26, second line. For "e're, read: e'er.
" 45, third line. Should read: *per fas et nefas*.
" 46, fortieth line. For "indeed no!" read: indeed, none!
" 55, sixteenth line. For "negatory," read: nugatory.
" 56, twenty-eighth line. Before "wisest," insert: best but the.
" 64, thirty-first line. For "Bothwell," read: Borthwick.
" 64, thirty-sixth line. For "Pittendriech," read: Pittendreich.

Appendix—Notes.

NOTE I. TO ACT III., SCENE III.—THE CASKET LETTERS, SONNETS, &c.

"HARPAGON.—Et cette CASSETTE comment est elle faite ?"
"MAITRE JACQUES.— . . . . . Elle est petite, si on le veut prendre par là ; mais je l'appelle grande pour ce qu' elle contient." MOLIÈRE.

Although the famous CASKET LETTERS, SONNETS, &c., from Mary to Bothwell are not mentioned in this Drama, because they were only discovered after the date of its action, ending with their separation at Carberry Hill, they must receive some notice, since the spirit and sentiments evident and expressed in them, are embodied in the conversations between Mary and Bothwell in the play. That these letters, &c., are genuine, the writer, after an examination of all accessible authorities, is as positive as a careful mortal examination and judgment can be.

"Some bold attempts have lately been made to prove these [the Casket] Letters and Sonnets to be forgeries; but, unfortunately for Mary's reputation, the principal arguments, in support of their authenticity, yet remain unanswered. 1. They were examined and compared with her acknowledged handwriting, in many letters to Elizabeth, not only by the English Commissioners, and by the Scottish Council and Parliament, but by the English Privy Council, assisted by several noblemen well affected to the cause of the Queen of Scots, who all admitted them to be authentic. (ANDERSON, Vol. IV.) This circumstance is of great weight in the dispute; for, although it is not very difficult to counterfeit a subscription, ☞ it is almost impossible to counterfeit any number of pages so perfectly as to elude detection. 2. Mary and her commissioners, by declining to refute the charge of the Regent, though requested to attempt a refutation in any manner or form, and told by Elizabeth that silence would be considered as the fullest confession of guilt, seemed to admit the justice of the accusation. (*Id ibid.*) 3. The Duke of Norfolk, who had been favored with every opportunity of examining the letters in question, and who gave the strongest marks of his attachment to the Queen of Scots, yet believed them to be authentic. ("State Trials," Vol. I.) 4. In the conferences between the Duke, Maitland of Lethington, and Bishop Lesley, all zealous partisans of Mary, the authenticity of the letters, and her participation in the murder of her husband, are always taken for granted. (*Id ibid.*) 5. *But, independent of all other evidence, the letters themselves contain many internal proofs of their authenticity; many minute and unnecessary particulars, which could have occurred to no person employed to forge them*, and which, as the English commissioners ingenuously observed, "were *unknown to any other than to herself and Bothwell.*" 6. *Their very indelicacy is a proof of their authenticity;* for although Mary, in an amorous moment, might slide into a gross expression, ☞ in writing to a man to whom she had sacrificed her honor, ☜ the framer of no forgery could hope to gain it credibility by imputing such expressions to so polite and accomplished a princess as the Queen of Scots. (Vol. I., p. 462, note 2. "History of Modern Europe." By William Russell, LL. D. Harper & Brothers, No. 82 Cliff Street, New York. 1833.)

NOTE II. DID MARY HAVE A CHILD BY BOTHWELL?

Absolute proofs and circumstantial evidence accumulate to prove that Mary Stuart had a child by Bothwell. Lord Mahon, a very careful and trustworthy historian, in his Review of the "*Lettres, Instructions et Memoires de Marie Stuart*," &c., &c., by Prince Alexander Labanoff, Article V., *Quarterly Review*, Vol. LXXVII., No. 153, London, 1846, page 139, &c., comes to the same conclusion as the Russian champion of the Queen, that she did have a daughter by Bothwell. Labanoff says, Vol. II., page 63, that this child was born in Lochleven Castle, in February, 1568, exactly, or about, nine months after her third marriage, 15th May, 1567.*

---

* 1567. 18th July. [Page 32.]—"The Lords of the Secret Council suggest to Mary the disavowal of her marriage with Bothwell. She refuses—being unable to consent to bastardize the infant of which she was then pregnant. See the letter from Throckmorton to Elizabeth, of 19th July, 1567. This letter, preserved in the British Museum (Cotton Mss., Caligula C. I., fol. 18), has been printed by Robertson. Appendix, No. XXII." * * *

1568. [Page 34.]—"In February Mary is delivered of a daughter, at Lochleven; the

Claude Nau, in his "History of Mary Stuart," edited by the Jesuit Joseph Stevenson, Edinburgh, 1883, pages 59–60, mentions her "lying on her bed, in a state of very great weakness, partly by reason of her great trouble (partly in consequence of a great flux, the result of a miscarriage of twins, her issue by Bothwell), so that she could move only with great difficulty."

This was the time that the miscreant Lindesay, the truculent Ruthven and Sir Robert Melville carried to Lochleven the Act of Abdication for Mary to sign. If Nau speaks the truth, and what reason had he for not doing so, the date must have been about 24th July, 1567. (Labanoff, II., 59.) Stevenson, in his lengthy Preface, pages clxxvii.–viii., a work in itself, is more explicit. These are his words, "Among the other revelations made to us by this [Nau's] narrative is one which takes us by surprise, the fact, namely, that shortly after her [Mary's] arrival in Lochleven, the Queen gave birth to twins, which, however, were still-born. Yet that such should have been the case might have been expected, for she herself declared that she was about to become a mother. Considering the rare intercourse which at this time took place between the ordinary household of the castle and the Queen's attendants, it is by no means incredible that the birth of these children was never known to the Laird of Lochleven and his family. It is never referred to in the correspondence of the period."

A note at the foot of the page, clxxvii., reads, "It must have occurred not long before 24th July" [1567]; that is in little more than two months

---

child is carried to France, where she eventually became a Nun in the Convent of our Lady at Soissons. The pregnancy of the Queen of Scotland has been denied by Gilbert Stuart, who wrote in 1782. But Dr. Lingard having reproduced this fact *as certain* in his 'History of England,' I have thought it right to adopt his account, supporting myself, moreover, by the testimony of Le Laboureur, an historian worthy of great credit, who, in his additions to the 'Memoirs of Castelnau' (Vol. L., p. 619, of the edition of 1731), speaks of the daughter of Mary Stuart. It must be remembered that the author whom I cite held an office of trust at the French court (he was the king's councillor and almoner), and that he had means of knowing several particulars long kept secret. Besides, when he published his work, it was easy for him to consult the registers of the Convent of our Lady at Soissons, and to assure himself if Mary's daughter had really been a nun there."—"Letters of Mary Stuart, Queen of Scotland, selected from the *Recueil des Lettres de Marie Stuart;* together with the Chronological Summary of Events during the Reign of the Queen of Scotland." By Prince Alexander Labanoff. Translated, with Notes and Introduction, by William Turnbull, Esq., Advocate, F. S. A. Scot. London : Charles Dolman, 61 New Bond Street. 1845.

after Mary and Bothwell were married, and justifies the argument of Prof. Schiern, that the marriage between Mary and Bothwell was precipitated in order to cover with the mantle of legitimacy, a child very likely the result of the double adultery of its parents.

Throckmorton, the English ambassador in Scotland, in a letter to Queen Elizabeth, under the date of 18th (19th) July, 1567, says, p. 142: "She [Mary] hath sent me word that she will rather dye, grounding herself upon thys reason that takynge herself to be seven weeks gon with chylde, by renouncynge Bothwell, she should acknowledge herselfe to be with chylde of a bastard, and to have forfayted her honoure, which she will not do to dye for it."

Even an experienced and observant woman does not know that she is with child, so as to speak decidedly, until several, certainly two months have elapsed. Consequently this child dates back to before the double marriage rites, 15th May, 1567, to justify any idea that the twins (referred to by Nau and Stevenson) were boy and girl, because some writers refer to a girl, and some to a boy. If there was any child, only one, the sex, female, is undoubted, but the tradition of a son born to Mary, in Lochleven Castle, of which the paternity was assigned to George Douglas, is mentioned by Burton (IV., 364-5; VII., 32, 43, 49, 129, 135). As to the daughter, see de Peyster's "Mary Stuart, a Study," pp. 99-100. " Bothwell and Mary Stuart," 112-114, 196-198. Rapin, Lingard, Froude, Mignet, and others, contain references to a daughter, and Miss Yonge wrote a novel, "Unknown to History," founded on the birth and career of an unfortunate female child. The distinction between the sexes is not recognizable until after, at least, three or four months of life in the embryo, consequently the reasons urged by Prof. Schiern, why Mary was desirous of precipitating her marriage with Bothwell, is fully explained. Lord Mahon, Burton, and all of the writers who argue out these stories, do so like lawyers carrying conviction. The discrepancies in the statement of the birth of that child, or those children, seem to be founded, *not* on the facts of the case, but the feelings of the chroniclers. Agnes Strickland, wishing to blacken the character of Bothwell, and to clear Mary from all stain, makes her "painful and dangerous" illness at Lochleven " exactly nine months from the period " Bothwell is said to have ravished her in Dunbar Castle.

Prince Labanoff makes the birth occur in February, 1568, nine months after Mary's public marriage. Nau, Laboureur, Castelnau, Throckmorton: the first, her secretary; the second, a priest of her communion; the third, a friend and invariably admitted to have been an honest man; and the fourth, a man who had nothing to gain by falsehood; all agree as to the pregnancy or the birth of a child or twins. Nau and Stevenson make the date six months earlier than Miss Strickland, and seven than Labanoff. The only doubtful point is the survival of a child. It was no uncommon thing to place royal children who were annoyances in conventical establishments, in contradistinction to the course of other monarchs, such as James V. of Scotland, Henry IV. and Louis XIV. of France, Charles II. of England, and others, who amply provided for their bastards, and ennobled them. That Mary's child, if a girl, had a different fate, is not surprising. It was at once a menace to the parties in power, and a victim to the hatred universally exhibited towards its father, Bothwell, and its mother, Mary. In all ages, to make way with such a birth, is neither extraordinary nor even unusual. To have done justice to such an unhappy fruit of an anlawful union would have been a rare exception to a detestable rule, almost invariable in its application.

To quote at large from Lord Mahon's critical Review of Mary's Letters, &c., it states that "Prince Labanoff admits, " (Vol. II., p. 68,) "*without hesitation*, the statement that Queen Mary, when sent to the Castle of Lochleven, in June, 1567, was with child by Bothwell, and that in February, 1568, she gave birth to a daughter, who was immediately removed to France, and became a Nun at the convent of Notre Dame, at Soissons." Considering the marriage of Mary to Bothwell, 15th May, 1567, it is obvious that her character is in no way affected by this tale, whether true or false. On this point, therefore, Prince Labanoff's prepossessions in her favor have no force, and the judgment of so well-informed and laborious an inquirer deserves, as we think, the greatest weight. *His assent to this tale* has led us to inquire the grounds on which it rests; and we shall now state what appear *the* testimonies in its favor, as well as the negative presumptions which may be raised against it. The statement rests mainly on the direct assertion of Le Laboureur, in his "Additions to the Memoires de Castelnau," and will be found at

Vol. I., p. 673, edition of 1659. Jean Le Laboureur (1562–75) is a writer of great research and accuracy. He is described by M. Weiss, in the *Biographie Universelle* [compare *Biographie Generale*, XXX., *de Firmin Didot* and *M. L. d'Hœfer*], as "*l'un des écrivains qui ont le plus contribué à éclaircir l'histoire de France.*" And as Prince Labanoff reminds us, he held a post of high confidence at the Court of France (*Conseiller et Aumônier du Roi*), and might become acquainted with many, until then very secret, transactions. But, if we believe, as appears most probably the case, that Le Laboureur derived the story from the manuscript notes and papers left behind by Castelnau, the evidence in its favor will appear stronger still. Michel de Castelnau, Seigneur de Mauvissiére (by which latter name he was commonly known during his life), had accompanied Mary, as French Ambassador to Scotland. In 1575 he was appointed French Ambassador in England ; and, as appears from Prince Labanoff's collection, became one of Mary's most frequent and most trusted correspondents. Castelnau says in his Memoirs, "*Elle est encore prisonnière sans pouvoir trouver moyen d'en sortir qu 'a l'instant il ne survienne quelques nouvelles difficultiés, les quelles ont pour la plupart passées par mes mains.*" (Vol. XXXIII., p. 357, in the collection of Petitot.) It appears also that, in the course of his diplomatic and political services, he had occasion to make many journeys through the north of France, and he might *not improbably, in one of them, have seen himself at Soissons, the unhappy offspring of a most ill-omened and most guilty marriage.* There is, however, a remarkable *confirmation* of Le Laboureur's story, wholly unknown to La Laboureur when he wrote, and not published until a century afterwards. It is contained in a secret dispatch from Throckmorton, the English Ambassador in Scotland, to his Queen, and will be found in the Appendix to Robertson's History, under date of July 18th, 1567. It appears the Ambassador had transmitted, by a secret channel, a proposal to Mary at Lochleven, that she should renounce Bothwell for her husband. But he adds, in his report to Elizabeth, "She hath sent me word that she will rather dye, grounding herself upon thys reason, that takyne herself to be *seven weeks* [embryo, consequently, about two months old] *gon* with chylde, by renouncynge Bothwell she should acknowledge herself to be with chylde of a bastard, and to have forfayted her honoure, which she will not do to dye for it." Physicians admit there is uncertainty in the symptoms of pregnancy previous to the fifth month, and, even later, the wisest and most observing are frequently deceived. Consequently, to speak so positively, Mary must have had more trustworthy evidence, and even this seems to establish Schiern's views as well as those of Nau and Stevenson.

Nor can it, on examination of the circumstances, be maintained that this answer was only a device of Mary to evade compliance. She must have foreseen that, as really happened, the renouncing of Bothwell would be again and again pressed upon her, and that if her first reason against it should, after some short interval, appear to be invalid she would then be unable to take a stand on any other ground. The concurrence of two such testimonies as Le Laboureur's in France and Throckmorton's in Scotland—each entitled to high confidence and each without the slightest knowledge of the other—would probably on most questions *be considered as decisive*.

"In this case, however, we have to set against them a strong *primâ facie* presumption on the other side—the utter silence as to this child at Soissons in all the correspondence of the period—the utter silence, first of Mary herself; secondly, of all her friends; and thirdly, of all her opponents. We propose to consider, under each of these heads, whether any sufficient ground for such silence can be assigned.

1. Mary herself had few opportunities of writing from her prison of Lochleven. Even the industry of Prince Labanoff is compelled to leave an utter blank between Sept. 3d, 1567, when Mary wrote to Sir Robert Melville, desiring him to 'send stuffs for clothes for herself and my maidens, for they are naked;' and March 31st, 1568, when we find two notes, one to Catharine de Medici and the other to the Archbishop of Glasgow, entreating speedy succor, and adding, "*je n'ose ecrire d'avantage.*" There are two other short notes from Lochleven, on the day preceding her escape, one to Catherine de Medici, and one to Elizabeth. In none of these could we expect to find any allusion to her pregnancy or to the birth of her child.

There is no letter at all from Mary during the hurried fortnight which elapsed between her escape from Lochleven and her arrival in England, except a few lines of doubtful authenticity dated from

Dundrennan, and addressed to Queen Elizabeth, which we think Prince Labanoff has too hastily admitted. (The authority he cites for it is only "*Marie Stuart, Nouvelle Historique,*" Paris, 1674. Moreover, the note from Dundrennan is not alluded to in the certainly authentic, letter which Mary addressed to Elizabeth from Workington only two days afterward.) This note, however, in no degree bears upon the present question. Within a very few weeks of her captivity in England, Mary became convinced of the horror with which her union with Bothwell was universally regarded. She consented, at the Conferences of York, that steps should be taken for the dissolution of her marriage and for the contracting of another with the Duke of Norfolk. From that time forward, therefore, we need not wonder that her letters should contain no allusion to the pledge of an alliance, which that pledge might, if known, render more difficult to dissolve, and which she knew was most hateful to all her well-wishers whether in France, in England, or in Scotland.

2. The same horror of this alliance and of its results may be thought an adequate motive for silence in such few of Mary's relatives or friends in France as must be supposed cognizant of the birth and existence of her daughter.

3. Of Mary's enemies, the first in power at this period was her illegitimate brother, the Earl of Murray, the Regent of Scotland. During a long time he professed a tender regard for his sister's reputation, and several times warned her against urging him to the public accusation which he made at last, on December 8th, 1568. It is, therefore, perfectly consistent with his professions and with his position that he should, in February, 1568, *have taken steps for the concealment of Mary's childbirth, and the sending of the infant to her relatives in France.* After December, 1568, there could no longer, indeed, be the slightest pretence to personal kindness and regard. But surely the chances of the royal succession would then supply him another and much stronger motive for concealment. In case the life of James VI.—a boy not yet three years old—should fail, Mary's daughter, if the marriage with Bothwell were legitimate, would become the next heir to the crown. A most perplexing question as to the strict validity of that marriage, and as to the rights of the true heir, would then arise.

It seems probable, therefore, in such a contingency, Murray and his associates in the secret had resolved to deny absolutely the fact of the birth or the existence of the infant.

The same motive for the greatest possible secrecy would have weight all through the life of the Nun at Soissons; but would cease at her death. And thus the same consideration would serve to explain both the silence observed during so many years, and the disclosure at last in Le Laboureur's annotation—always supposing the secret to have been confined, both in Scotland and in France, to extremely few and trusty persons.

We offer these conjectures as, in our mind, greatly diminishing, though not, we admit, entirely removing the force of the objections against the story. *And on the whole, looking to the positive testimonies in its favor, we certainly incline, with Prince Labanoff, to a belief in its* TRUTH."

NOTE III. MARY AND KIRKALDY OF GRANGE.

The most careful analytical study of the character of Mary leads the unprejudiced critic, up or down, to the consistent judgment of the calm historian, Lord Mahon, "the strength of her passions ruined all;" hers "was an emotional nature, as ardent as it was unscrupulous." "Judicious calmness will not allow him [Burton, a fair and unprejudiced writer] to violate historic facts in order to impart a fictitious innocence to a sadly perverted and vitiated character." "*When she was not under the influence of the violent attachments to which she afterwards yielded* [1563–5]. Burton observes, in another place (IV., 95), "and while she views her marriage as a political arrangement, she scorned anything but a thoroughly great alliance." Yet she had been in love with Damville, and to him, in her favor, succeeded Chastelard, Sir John Gordon, and then the miserable Darnley. Every just critic will reject the imputation in regard to Rizzio, although it is very doubtful if he was the repulsive creature generally represented, but rather an insinuating, not unattractive man. "The beautiful Mary was, in reality, one of the most abandoned and unscrupulous of her sex." These are terrible extracts; each word seems to be wet with blood and stained with passion. Mary's conduct at Carberry Hill is utterly inexplicable, unless we accept as correct the definition of the arch-poet: "It [Love] is to be all made of *fantasy* ["passion, wishes" or desires], said the arch-expression-dissector, "Love [such as that of Mary Stuart] is not altogether a delirium, yet it has many points in common therewith;" and, remarks another celebrated critic, unless the idea of Burton is conceded as the true solution, "The latent resolution [of Kirkaldy to betray his party] was planted in his heart by the siren [Mary Stuart] when she chose to surrender to him [at Carberry Hill and abandon Bothwell to his fate]. She may have been carried away by a sudden flood of feeling, as she certainly was instantly captured by the exterior graces and accomplishments of Darnley. Finally, not to weary the reader with arguments, however powerful and pertinent, the question presents itself: Would Lindesay, "the bloodiest and most furious that could be found in the whole troop" (Stevenson, clxxix.), if he did not believe that he had guaged her nature, have dared to make her the proposition, in Lochleven Castle, that "he would free her if she would love him?" (Nau, 59.)

Lindesay afterward became one of her partisans. She was a veritable Circe. Again, would Ruthven have dared to commit a like offense without some excuse? "Ruthven, who had been commissioned to reside within the [Lochleven] Castle [with Lindesay] as her keepers," "was removed in consequence of having been guilty of an act of scandalous indecency. Early one morning he came into the bedroom of his captive and made indecent proposals to her; offering to procure her liberty at the payment of her sin." (Stevenson, clxxviii.)

Ruthven, like Lindesay, afterward joined her party (Nau, 59). These relations tally with the curious story told by Michelet of Margaret of Valois, another royal lady of peculiar temperament and passionate nature.

Margaret of Valois had innumerable lovers, and especially her brothers, the King, Henry III., and the Duke of Alencon, a candidate for the hand of Elizabeth of England. Henry III., who survived her, was not less jealous of her; was more husband than her real husband, the spiritual and patient King of Navarre, afterwards Henry IV. Margaret's lover, for the time being, was the famous duelist, Bussy of Amboise, of whom the king's favorite du Guast was at once accuser, or informer and persecutor. On the 30th of October, 1575, Margaret determined upon a decided step, and demonstrated that she was the true sister of the King, Charles IX., the hero of St. Bartholomew's day. She looked up an assassin. In the Convent of the Augustins, a certain Baron of Viteaux was in hiding, who had killed, among others, one of the immediate circle of Henry III. Had it not been for du Guast, this king who had a short memory could have been easily worked upon to pardon Viteaux. Consequently Viteaux detested du Guast. Margaret did not hesitate to seek out this man of blood, either in the cloister, or more probably the vast and dark church in which he kept himself concealed. This was in the night before All Souls Day, and the occasion was favorable. All the church bells of the capital were clanging in chorus, and the Parisians having passed the whole day in frequenting churches and visiting tombs, had sought their homes early. Margaret availed herself of these circumstances, so opportune to her occasion. Trembling and shuddering, she asked Viteaux to do for her sake that which he himself desired to do for his own. Viteaux nevertheless, fought shy, and did not wish to do the deed gratis: if tradition is reliable. She promised; he required immediate settlement. It was night, and all the numerous dead, in this church full of sepulchres, awaiting their annual festival, were not more peaceable and unconcerned than the sleeping living. The intrepid little woman paid cash down. Her man kept his bargain: du Guast was killed the next day. (Michelet, X., V., 82.)

Ruthven expected the same sort of pay, but Mary did not see it in the same light as Margaret. Perhaps she did not trust her Scotchman and did not believe he would or could carry out the contract.

NOTE IV. MAITLAND OF LETHINGTON.

"Thenceforward, therefore, we see a double current where before there had been but a single stream. Murray became the head of the religious party; Maitland of Lethington of the political; and the distinction of the ends which they proposed to themselves soon widened the separation between them.

"Maitland, *who cared as much for religion as politicians are usually apt to care*, discovered in the disputed title of Elizabeth to her crown, and in the right to it which had been advanced for his own Queen, an opportunity of re-establishing Scotland on its old equality with its old rival, and perhaps for a splendid repayment of old scores and grudges. Intrigue was his proper element. Life was a game in which he was mainly interested as an exercise of political ability, and the 'situation' had irresistible attractions for him. No sooner was Mary returned than she found in him the most efficient minister of her ambition. He threw himself into all her schemes, and gave them shape and consistency; and in a few years he had sown the seeds of disaffection over the whole northern counties of England. He parried Elizabeth's demand for a ratification of the Treaty of Edinburgh (in which it had been stipulated that Mary should formally renounce her claim) by a counter-demand that she should be acknowledged as her successor; and Elizabeth's refusal, which the circumstances of the case rendered inevitable, he was able to display as a national affront in the eyes of the proud and foolish nobility. Everything prospered with him. A dexterous flattery had dissolved the Protestant League; Murray was almost the only nobleman who openly adhered to it; and in the atmosphere of suspicion which Maitland had contrived to create, a coldness had arisen even towards Murray among the ministers of the Kirk. The Darnley marriage was probably Maitland's devising; for Mary's title was doubly fortified by it, and at once upon its taking place a large section of the English transferred their allegiance to her. The northern counties were ready to rise in the summer of 1565, and the attempt would not long have been delayed if Darnley's own wretched character had not ruined everything. No one could trust him, and yet it was impossible to act without him; and at the end of a year, it was found indispensably necessary, unless their entire policy was to fall in pieces, that in some way or other he should be got rid of. Maitland was the first person who suggested the Murder to the Queen; and if she could have left it to him as he desired, the thing would have been done skillfully and quietly, and Darnley would have disappeared out of life with as little disturbance as a thousand other poor princes had caused in disappearing who have been in the way of politicians. Maitland had been responsible for his introduction upon the stage, and like a good subject he was ready to do his best to remedy the evil which he had caused. *Disappointment is a feeble word for the feeling with which he must have regarded the sub-*

stitution of Bothwell for himself, and the sacrifice of an empire for a miserable love intrigue. Everything was ruined irretrievably; and, although, even after Carberry Hill, *Maitland undertook if she would promise to surrender Bothwell, to restore her Crown, yet her refusal convinced him that her cause was for the time hopeless,* and he consented with the rest of the nobles to her deposition and imprisonment in Lochleven. She had committed herself in every way; even on paper; in letters of her own handwriting; and though such men as Maitland find little difficulty in forgiving crimes, blunders, gross patent blunders, are without excuse. Accordingly, as long as she remained in Scotland, he now kept himself comparatively in the background, doing little or nothing, but formally acting with his old friends, and supporting Murray. In the autumn of 1568, however, a new complication brought around fresh opportunities, and the old hopes grew green again. Murray's regency was secretly detestable to him—a very solecism in government, unendurable by a philosophical statesman. As long as it lasted the moral law was the law of the land. Sins were punished as crimes, and political difficulties were resolved by a stupid and unstatesmanlike appeal to the 'Word of God.' *Such a state of things was an affront to his very creed, and an outrage on his understanding.* Self preservation is the first law of life; and if theories such as these obtained currency what would be the use of the Maitlands? His national pride was further irritated at the position in which Mary had been placed by Elizabeth, who had compelled her to plead at an English tribunal; his jealousy was alarmed by the evident anxiety of the English Government to get the young King into their hands; and Mary herself was now in a country where the evidence of her guilt was less notorious, and where it was possible to deny it. Bothwell was safe out of the way in a Danish prison, and she immediately on her arrival in England had been welcomed by a powerful party, who were secretly ready to recognise her as the representative of the Catholic cause. All these things combined to revive the old schemes; and Murray, when summoned to York to meet the English commissioners, had already seen so much cause to distrust Maitland that he was afraid to leave him behind and had joined him with himself in the commission.

"Perhaps he had already been in secret correspondence with Mary; at any rate, he was no sooner in York, than he placed himself in correspondence with her, and privately directed her in the course which she was to pursue in defending herself. But the worst mischief which Maitland could have done in Scotland was small in comparison with that which his visit to England gave him the opportunity of effecting. Whatever admiration is due to audacity and skill must be given him without stint for the scheme which he now conceived. The Duke of Norfolk, who had been sent to York as the President of the English commission, was the first English subject, the premier nobleman in the peerage. Professing himself to be a Protestant, his allegiance to the Reformation was as hollow as that of the mass of the nobility. If Mary Stuart could be married to *him*, and if he would support her title to the crown, her success, Maitland considered, would be certain. * * *

"It was a really magnificent scheme. Although it failed, there is something grand even in failure on such a scale; and Maitland must have the credit as well as the responsibility of the entire conception."

Fraser's Magazine, Vol. 42, p. 537-8.

Decay.

"THE WORD! Do you remember, Meister? I told you then, that you had found the right one.   *   *   But you look like a happy man, and to what do you owe it? *To the Word*, the only right word: 'Art!'"

He let her finish the sentence, then answered gravely:

"There is still a loftier word, noble lady! Whoever owns it is rich indeed. He will no longer wander—seek in doubt." "And this is?" she asked incredulously, with a smile of superior knowledge.

"I have found it," he answered firmly. "It is 'LOVE!'"

Sophonisba bent her head, saying softly and sadly, "Yes, yes; Love!"

GEORGE EBER'S "*A Word, only a Word*," page 348.

"*But, mortal pleasure, what art thou in truth!*
THE TORRENT'S SMOOTHNESS ERE IT DASH BELOW."
CAMPBELL.

"Discarding modern historians, who in too many instances do not seem to entertain the slightest scruple in dealing with the memory of the dead."   *   *   *   "*I am not ashamed to own that I have a deep regard for the memory of* [BOTHWELL] *Lord Dundee—a regard founded on the firm belief in his public and private virtues, his high and chivalrous honor, and his unshaken loyalty to his sovereign.* But those feelings, however strong, would never lead me to vindicate an action of wanton and barbarous cruelty, or even attempt to lessen the stigma by a frivolous or dishonest excuse. No cause was ever effectually served by mean evasion, any more than it can be promoted by unblushing exaggeration or by gross perversion of facts."

WM. E. AYTOUN, "*Regarding John Graham, of Claverhouse, Viscount of Dundee.*"

"Women are the priestesses of Predestination."   D'ISRAELI'S "*Coningsby.*"

"The man who [like Bothwell] anticipates his century is always persecuted when living and is always pilfered [robbed of his credit] when dead." D'ISRAELI'S "*Vivian Gray.*"

"*With him his Fortune played as with a ball,*
She first has tossed him up, and now she lets him fall."
Verses on Medallion of COUNT GRIFFENFELD, *Royal Library, Copenhagen.*

"*He will surely violently turn and toss thee like a* BALL *into a large country* [or as in the margin, 'the captivity of a man']: there shalt thou die, and there the chariots of thy glory shall be the shame of thy lord's house. And I will drive thee from thy station, and from thy state shall he pull thee down." [What could be more apposite to the end of Bothwell than these verses.]   ISAIAH, xxii., 18, 19.

"The black earth yawns, the mortal disappears."

TENNYSON'S "*Ode on the Death of the Duke of Wellington.*"

1   1

O anticipate, for the purpose of making a point, Bothwell's enemies depict him—the Hereditary Lord High Admiral of his native realm, born in one of the grandest ancestral strongholds and castellated mansions in Clydesdale; the theme of the historian, the poet and the minstrel; celebrated in the words of a ditty known during the Crusades, from the Atlantic to the Dead Sea,

"Bothwell Bank thou bloomest fair"—

Bothwell Castle on the Clyde.

as dying a maniac in chains, in a loathsome Danish cell. This statement is founded on malice, forgery and ignorance. Notwithstanding all the efforts of individuals and governments, of learning and industry, a screen, as impenetrable as the "Veil of Isis," fell over the last years of "the great" "Scotland's proudest Earl." His principal advocate, Petrick, says, "*Then suddenly*—(referring to the autumn of 1571)—ALL IS SILENT! a great gap of four years occurs:—for what reason?" There is a solution and a plausible one. For six years the Danish government "had been tormented by the demands of Queen Elizabeth [of England] and the [successive] Regents of Scotland for the deliverance of Bothwell into their hands." Worn out with communications, reclamations and declamations, Frederic II. "allowed the report of Bothwell's death to be circulated, and so put an end to all the worry on the subject." This accounts for the doubts as to whether Bothwell died in 1575, according to Petrick, or in 1577 or 1578, according to Schiern and others. One sad fact is certain. He realized the words of the Prophet, Isaiah, xv., 9-10, in regard to the once mighty Belshazzar, "Thou shalt not be joined with them [thy forefathers and thy peers] in burial." Belted Earl and husband of a queen, his corpse rests in an unknown grave and foreign land. Bothwell, from the fall of 1567 until his decease—whenever it occurred—was "a prisoner of Hope" in the hands of Frederic II., King of Denmark. This monarch was a curious character. He was at once the protector of Bothwell and his custodian—whether at the last a severe or a lenient jailor nothing is definitely known. Falsehoods on the subject have been propagated industriously, but nothing trustworthy. That Frederic allowed him, for years, pocket money, respectful attendance, company and correspondence, and sufficient means to dress in accordance with his rank and enjoy good cheer is certain. In November, 1567, the king styles Bothwell "Our particular Favorite" (Shiern, 332). In January, 1568, Bothwell was living in Copenhagen, without anxieties for the future. When transferred to Malmo, it was still a sort of honorable confinement. His apartment was stately for the time. Even after this,

Malmo-huus.

down to 1571, velvet and silk were furnished for his attire, and his residence in Malmo, except as to duress, was anything but derogatory. He was purely a prisoner of State and of consideration. It was not until the 16th of June, 1573, that he was transferred to Dragsholm. Even then, it is very doubtful if his confinement was as strict as represented. It is questionable if his treatment in Zealand was more rigorous or galling than that of Mary in England. According to inspiration, Jeremiah was promised again and again, as the recompense for his own unmerited sufferings, undergone in obedience to his call, that his life should be spared. "Thy life shall be as a prey unto thee; because thou hast put thy trust in me, saith the Lord." If life is a boon, and if the wise king was justified in saying, "A living dog is better than a dead lion"—in that while there is Life there is Hope—Bothwell was certainly better off in comfort and safety in Denmark than either one of his enemies perishing in their prime and power by violent ends—deaths* culminating in horror with the burning alive at the stake of the Scottish Lion King at Arms; sacrificed thus on his return to Scotland from his mission to Denmark to solicit the extradition of Bothwell, because on the voyage home he had learned too much of the villainy of Murray and his associates. A moral lesson is conveyed by a time-table presenting the miserable and often horrible manner in which those who persecuted Bothwell went to their last account. It is very comfort-

---

* It is more than remarkable how every one, of greater or lesser note, who persisted in aspiring to the hand of Mary, came to grief. The most extraordinary instance is that of Erik, King of Sweden, who, on hearsay evidence, became completely enamored of her, and made expensive preparations for a voyage to Scotland to prosecute his suit in person. But the fate of her other admirers came to him, and he ended his life, after many weary woeful years of imprisonment in a vile dungeon, by poison in a plate of pea-soup.

ing to his friends and admirers to learn this. The author has derived the greatest satisfaction from the investigation of each successive terrible and untimely catastrophe.

Extracts from Marryat's "Jutland and the Danish Isles" [Vol. I., 408-19], appended as a Note to subsequent pages, will serve to present a mingling of fact and fable in regard to Bothwell's last imprisonment and sepulture, which is about as true as tradition* generally is—that is to say, there is a basis of fact, but the superstructure is almost all fable.

---

* Scarcely any man living has had opportunities more ample than the author to become acquainted with the untrustworthiness of popular tradition. In tracing back the history of a neighborhood it was painful to observe the discrepancies manifested in the recollections of the "oldest inhabitant" in contiguous localities. "MEMORY IS ATTENTION," and it is seldom that individuals pay attention to anything that is not of immediate personal interest to themselves. All the passions and all the weaknesses influence memory. People hear what their elders gabble, then talk the matter over and garble it to suit themselves, and transmit a tissue in which truth is like the Bean in a huge "Twelfth Cake." The bean is there, but a hundred slices may be cut before one reveals its presence. The author once sought out a road which, about seventy years since, was a main route between two frequented settlements, one a little port. A number had heard of it, a dozen pointed out depressions which indicated where it must have been located, but only one man could trace it. Why? In his youth he had worked upon it. No one but the author had ever thought it worthy of inquiry. The informant is extremely aged, the investigator is over sixty; in a few years both will have passed away, and after them everything in regard to the case in question will be mere surmise. So it is as to the last days of Bothwell. Horace Marryat advances as a proof that the corpse, which he claims to be Bothwell's, was really so—"a pearl embroidered cushion [pillow], a mark of rank," among the dead of the sixteenth century, "was found in the Scottish earl's

In permitting Bothwell to leave her at Carberry Hill—when the winning cards were still in her hands and retreat to Dunbar was by no means hopeless, nor even uncertain (Wiesener, 408)*—with reinforcements coming up, which

---

coffin." Even this is apocryphal—mere report, as worthless as tradition ever turns out to be. As "belted Earl," as mighty Magnate, as Hereditary Lord High Admiral of a realm, as Lieutenant General and military *Alter Ego* of a sovereign, as her husband, he was "the observed of all observers!"

"'Tis 'great' to hear the passer by say, There he goes! That's he!" Greatness in a measure is proved when "the world is singling you out and indicating you." As a prisoner, in a foreign land, in a remote castle, on a sea-surrounded islet, Bothwell was buried alive, forgotten.

* That Bothwell, with his acknowledged ability, could have effected a retreat to Dunbar, a fortress impregnable to everything the Rebel Lords could have brought, or kept, together against it, which in itself alone would have insured ultimate success, is demonstrable by a hundred parallel operations. (*Declaration of the Earl of Bothwell, addressed to the King of Denmark.* Agnes Strickland's "Letters of Mary Queen of Scots," II., 324) .All it required was military ability, coolness and intrepidity. He possessed all three (see pages 48-'9, *supra*). The Queen's Body Guard, of Hackbutteers, the men-at-arms of David Home of Wedderburn and of John of Blackadder, Bothwell's own Borderers and the three falconets (light field artillery) with their "constables," would have been amply sufficient to cover a withdrawal of less than twenty miles, especially after impending night set in. The effect upon a fight, at this date, of a few trained musketeers, was almost incalculable. With a few efficient cavalry in support they could have turned this "Black" Sabbath into a bright Sunday. Witness the victory won, in a disadvantageous position on the Gelt, near Naworth Castle, in Cumberland, England, 19th February, 1570, by Lord Hunsdon over Lord Dacre. The latter had 5,000 certainly as good troops as the "Bonded" Lords; the former 1,500, but among these were the trained "Berwick harquebussmen." The volleys of the latter staggered and demoralized the bold Dacre Borderers, horse and foot, and then Hunsdon fell on them with a

would have assured a victory to Mary, this determination of the Queen to separate her fortunes from her husband has always, and in some degree, justly been brought for-

---

squadron of horse—such as those under Wedderburn and Blackadder at Carberry Hill—and the rebel armament "went to water." To show the effect of coolness coupled with capacity, recall an incident in the life of Sir Andrew Murray of BOTHWELL, son of the favorite colleague of Wallace, Regent of Scotland. "He was in the Highlands, in 1336, with a small body of followers, when the King of England came upon him with an army of twenty thousand. The Regent heard the news, but, being then about to hear mass, did not permit his devotions to be interrupted. When the mass was ended, the people around him pressed him to order a retreat : 'There is no haste,' said Murray, composedly. At length his horse was brought out, he was about to mount, and all expected that the retreat was to commence. But the Regent observed that a strap of his armor had given way, and this interposed new delays. He sent for a particular coffer, out of which he took a piece of skin, and cut and formed with his own hand, and with much deliberation, the strap which he wanted. By this time, the English were drawing very near, and, as they were so many in number, some of the Scottish knights afterwards told the historian who narrates the incident, that no space of time ever seemed so long to them as that which Sir Andrew employed in cutting that thong of leather. Now, if this had been done in a mere vaunting or bragging manner, it would have been the behaviour of a vain-glorious fool. But Sir Andrew Murray had already fixed upon the mode of his retreat, and he knew that every symptom of coolness and deliberation which he might show would render his men steady and composed in their turn, from beholding the confidence of their leader. He at length gave the word, and, putting himself at the head of his followers, made a most masterly retreat, during which the English, notwithstanding their numbers, were unable to obtain any advantage over him, so well did the Regent avail himself of the nature of the ground."

A parallel to this is the British General Crawford's coolness, during the Peninsular War, under Wellington, in Spain, in quietly

ward as an argument that she had ceased to love him, if she ever did care passionately for him.* Here once more Mary's principal biographer and advocate can be cited against herself and client, admitting (II., 83–'4) that the Queen could be "ungrateful and unreasonable," subject to "strange infatuations;" "had taken her resolution"—devoid of common sense, and blind and deaf to the les-

---

stopping his retreat to trice up and flog delinquents in face of the superior forces of the pursuing French, pressing hard upon his rear guard, and so close upon him that spent shots sometimes fell among those present at the punishment. Sir Henry Clinton, the Royal Commander against the Colonies, 1777-82, owed his rise and rank to his successful retreat with a comparative handfull, in the face of the French, during the "Seven Years' War" in Germany; and the same was the case with the noble Fraser, killed, under Burgoyne, in the Battle of Bemis Heights or Second Saratoga, 7th October, 1777. Had he survived, and if Burgoyne had listened to his advice, the wrecks of the invading force might have been able to withdraw into Canada, under the cover of the famous Light Infantry, which Fraser knew how to handle so admirably. The military murder by Morgan's sharpshooters forbade the experiment. Lord Clive, one of the greatest born-generals who ever illustrated the Annals of War, gained all his successes in India—such as Arcot, Arnee, Cowerepauk, Seviavaram, Plassey, &c.—victories which laid the basis of the vast dominion of Great Britain in that Asian peninsula—against greater odds than Bothwell had to contend with, even after his Militia—Temporary or Feudal Levies—had failed him and flunked.

*Mary "was impulsive, hot-headed, warm-hearted, and in her virtues and her faults essentially a woman. *She fell over head and ears in love with Bothwell*, and, as is often the case when this occurs to a woman, allowed her individuality to be absorbed in his, and became for a time a mere tool in his hands. With the exception of this episode, she conducted herself very properly." ("Mary and Elizabeth," in *Truth*, London, Thursday, 11th January, 1883.)

sons of experience—"before she asked advice." If she had only shown a small portion of the energy she displayed eight months before, when, in the rough autumn weather, through a difficult country, and dangerous population, she rode on horseback fifty miles, thither from Jedburgh and back to visit her lover, previously wounded in her service, in Hermitage Castle—his headquarters as Warden of the

Hermitage Castle.

Marches, (see article "Jedburgh Abbey," *Saturday Review*, 30th September, 1882, page 439), Carberry Hill would have been a decisive triumph, instead of a disastrous and disgraceful catastrophe. It was simply the effect of cause; the inevitable quantities uniting in the product: *Ate* and Fate! If readers would study the most flattering stories of her friends in the light of reason, not feeling, they would find enough therein, to condemn their heroine and absolve Bothwell. Froude's (VII., 369) exposition of her character is masterly, and its correctness is established more and more by comparison and investigation. If this stood alone there would be difficulty in meeting it.*

Rarely, perhaps, has any woman combined in herself so many noticeable qualities as Mary Stuart; with a feminine insight into men and things and human life, she had cultivated herself to that high perfection in which accomplishments were no longer advantitious ornaments, but were wrought into her organic constitution. Though luxurious in her ordinary habits, she could share in the hard field-life of the huntsman or the soldier with graceful cheerfulness; she had vigor, energy, tenacity of purpose, with perfect and never-failing self-possession (?) and, as the one indispensable foundation for the effective use of all other qualities, she had indomitable courage. She wanted none either of the faculties necessary to conceive a great purpose, or of the abilities necessary to execute it, except, perhaps, only this—that while she made politics the game of her life, it was

---

* To show how fallible, after all, Agnes Strickland—the accepted biographer *par excellence* of Mary, Queen of Scots—proves herself to be, page 119, Note 1, Vol. III., of her "Letters of Mary, Queen of Scots," she states that Bothwell was the author [of the French translation] of the *Latin Libel* (upon Mary) of Buchanan, styled his "*Detectio.*" Such a mistake is not only wicked, inexcusable and absurd, but not more so than many of the epithets Miss Strickland applies to Bothwell and her inconsistent remarks upon him. When this "*Detectio*" appeared, Bothwell was already a captive in Denmark, and no one charges him, after that period, with any reflection upon his ill-fated but false consort.

a game only [like the battles of Pyrrhus], though played for a high stake. *In the deeper and nobler emotions she had neither share nor sympathy.* Here lay the vital difference of character between the Queen of Scots and her great rival, and here was the secret of the difference of their fortunes. In intellectual gifts Mary Stuart was at least Elizabeth's equal; and Anne Boleyn's daughter, as she said herself, was "no angel." But Elizabeth could feel like a man an unselfish interest in a great cause; Mary Stuart *was ever her own centre of hope, fear or interest. She thought of nothing, cared for nothing, except as linked with the gratification of some ambition, some desire, some humor of her own,* and thus Elizabeth was able to overcome temptations before which Mary fell.   *   *   While her sister of England was trifling with an affection for which foolish is too light an epithet, Mary Stuart, when scarcely more than a girl, was about to throw herself alone into the midst of the most turbulent people in Europe, fresh emerged out of revolution, and loitering in the very rear of civilization; she going among them to use her charms as a spell to win them back to the Catholic Church, to weave the fibres of a conspiracy from the Orkneys to the Lands End; prepared to wait, to control herself, to hide her purpose till the moment came to strike, yet with a purpose fixed as the stars to trample down the Reformation, and to seat herself at last on Elizabeth's throne.

"Whatever policy," said Randolph of her, "is in all the chief and best-practiced heads in France, whatever craft, falsehood or deceit is in all the subtle brains of Scotland, is either fresh in this woman's memory or she can fette it with a wet finger." (Froude, VII., 369.)

She was deluded by Kirkaldy, as she had often been before by Murray; but her first act, after she discovered the awful mistake she had made in disregarding her husband's counsels, was to write to him, and send him a purse or sum of gold. She again wrote to him from Lochleven; she refused to separate her fortunes from his; her thoughts dwelt constantly upon him; and the very night of her escape from Lochleven, "while the men were stretching their aching legs, Mary Stuart was writing letters." To whom? To her uncle, the Cardinal of Lorraine, in Paris, for assistance, and to her lover and husband, Bothwell. She sent the Laird of Ricarton, a kinsman of Bothwell, to raise the Hepburns, united to the "great Earl" by family and feudal ties, and make a dash on Dunbar to secure a port for the arrival of himself and of succor from France, and, when that port of entry was secured, to go on to Bothwell and tell him that she was free. Bothwell himself wrote to Frederic that he was on his way to Scotland, to raise men and money, when he was "treacherously captured" in Carmo-sund. Ricarton did "go on," and found Bothwell in his confinement at Malmo. Another account says, as soon as she breathed the air of freedom, she despatched a messenger to find Bothwell, wherever he might be, and announce the happy tidings of her release, and summon him to her side, whence he never should have been permitted, for her security and honor, to depart. Agnes Strickland, color blind as to every shade which could relieve or glorify the portrait of Bothwell, says that on her flight from Langside, Lord

Herries wanted Mary to take refuge in Earlston Castle, a stronghold belonging to Bothwell; that Mary became greatly agitated, burst into tears, and refused, "as if fearing to encounter her evil genius in his form, and prefering to brave any other peril than that of meeting him again." This is a puerile idea, and unworthy anything but the pen of a woman fighting to rehabilitate one of her sex, and, in so doing, so bitterly prejudiced as to forget the very characteristics of a such peculiar specimen of her sex as Mary. Consistent with their nature, it is likely Mary's love for Bothwell was so strong in her bosom, that she could not bear to tread the halls without him that once she had trodden with him in happier days. There is no greater "suffering"—exclaims Dante—"than to recall past happiness amid present wretchedness." Finally, to demonstrate the fallacy, if not wickedness, of all this misrepresentation of Mary's feelings for Bothwell to screen and excuse the Queen, even as late as the spring of 1571, when she was at Sheffield, she was in correspondence with him in Malmo, and had written, herself, to Frederic II., entreating him not to listen to the pursuasion of the Scottish envoy, Buchanan, laboring with so much enmity and earnestness against her husband. The correspondence must have been patent, for Buchanan told Cecil that, "if he took the trouble, he might intercept some of her letters."

That Lord Boyd, in 1569, obtained Bothwell's consent to the dissolution of his marriage, to enable Mary to marry

Norfolk, shows that the intercourse between the Earl and Queen, by letter and messenger, was still permitted. The fact is, Frederic's whole treatment of Bothwell was regulated by the probabilities of Mary's restoration to her throne. It was not until her case seemed desperate that Bothwell was finally immured, if he was ever actually thrown into a dungeon, which is very questionable.

What became of Bothwell after they parted, forever on earth, at Carberry Hill, Sunday, 15th June, 1567, is soon told. He returned unmolested to Dunbar, and remained there for several weeks undisturbed, although he did not confine himself to the fortress, but cruised about in the Frith of Forth, even penetrating beyond Edinburgh to the neighborhood of Linlithgow, to hold a meeting with Lord Claude Hamilton. Of his political projects at this time no record remains. Confiding the defence of Dunbar to his kinsman, Sir Patrick Whitlaw, he sailed thence, in the beginning of July, with two light vessels, and steered northward to visit his brother-in-law, Huntley, at Strathbogie Castle, about ten miles south-by-west of Banff, to the eastward of the Moray Frith. His intention was, doubtless, to raise forces in the northeast and renew the struggle. The Queen had many friends in that quarter; adherents who did join her after her escape from Lochleven, next year, 1568, and fought for her at Langside. Thence he proceeded to Spynie Castle, just north of Elgin, the residence of his aged great-uncle, Patrick Hep-

burn, Bishop of Murray, by whom he was brought up.
Here a project was entertained to murder Bothwell, and
a proposition to this effect was made to the English
ambassador, Sir Nicholas Throckmorton, at Edinburgh.
Whether the offer was rejected from policy or morality
is not clearly shown. Some difficulty occurred, and Bothwell is charged with having slain one of his illegitimate
cousins, who, in conjunction with two Rokebys, English
spies incited by greed, were plotting against him. The
latter even offered to kill the Bishop as well as the Earl.
Throckmorton seems to have objected to such a summary
proceeding, because no advantage could be derived from
the crime in favor of England and Elizabeth.

Bothwell now determined to visit his dukedom of the
Orkneys, and sailed for the chief town of the group,
Kirkwall. The opinion of those who have investigated
the matter with most attention is that Bothwell—after his
failure to enlist the active co-operation of his brother-in-law,
Huntley—intended to proceed to the Orkneys, gather what
strength he could, and then, by the way of Sweden, proceed to France to arouse the sympathies of Charles IX.—
who, personally, was very friendly to him, and had confidence in the Earl based on his service as "Chamberlain" at one time, and as "Captain of the Royal Scottish
Body Guard," at another,—and derive from France, not
only "the sinews of war," money, but actual military
assistance. Fate, however, traversed all Bothwell's bold

projects, and, at Kirkwall, he was received with the treachery he had always experienced from those he had benefited. His castellan, Gilbert Balfour, brother of Sir James Balfour, who had betrayed him after his marriage, and delivered up Edinburgh Castle to the Rebels—both accomplices in the murder of Darnley—turned the cannons of the place upon his feudal lord and benefactor. In consequence of this, Bothwell remained only two days in the port of Kirkwall, and then sailed northward to the Shetlands. Here he met with better treatment. The Bailiff, Olaf Sinclair, was a kinsman of the Earl's (now Duke) mother, Jane Sinclair. Olaf received him kindly, and the people furnished him supplies—a gratuity which was afterwards made the excuse for an onerous tax. Meanwhile, 19th August, Kirkaldy of Grange, Murray of Tullibardine and the Bishop of Orkney, who had married Mary to Bothwell, sailed from Dundee with four ships of war, the best in Scotland, which, in addition to the seamen, carried four hundred picked arquebusiers (musketeers) as marines. The three commanders had authority to bring Bothwell, if taken, to a summary trial, and execute him. On the 25th August, 1567, the four pursuing ships sailed into Bressay Sound, on the shore of which stands Lerwick, the principal town of the Shetland group. At this date, Bothwell's squadron consisted of four small vessels, two of which he had brought from Dunbar, and two Hanseatic armed Pinks, "two-masted lesser war ships," which he had hired at Sumburgh Head. One of these was named the "Pelican." Unconscious of danger, Bothwell's ships lay at anchor, and a large portion of their crews were on shore. Bothwell, himself, at the time was a guest of the Bailiff, Olaf Sinclair. Those in command who had remained on board, cut their cables and put to sea, and made their way to Unst, the most northerly of the Shetlands. In his pursuit, Kircaldy ran his flagship, the "Unicorn," on a rock, and it went down. Bothwell, meanwhile, made his way by land to the Yell Sound, and thence by water to Unst, where he rejoined his ships. Thence he sent back one vessel to pick up his men who had been left on shore. With the other three he was overtaken, in the last days of August, by Kircaldy with his three remaining ships of war. A hard fight ensued, which lasted for many hours. In the course of it the mainmast of Bothwell's best ship was carried away by a cannon shot, and the south-west wind swelling into a fierce gale put an end to the conflict by dispersing the combatants. The Earl was driven with two of his vessels out into the North Atlantic, and one was captured. Running south-east-by-east before the quartering gale, Bothwell soon traversed the 250 miles of ocean which separated the Shetlands from Norway, and first made the Island of Carmoe, twenty miles north-west of Stavanger, and was piloted into the quiet waters of Carm or Carmoe Sound. The ships had scarcely cast anchor when the Dano-Norwegian ship-of-war "Bjornen," Captain Christern Aalborg, made its appearance. By this Aalborg, Bothwell was "treacherously captured," and carried into the port of Bergen. There his case was investigated by a commission or jury, composed of four-and-twenty principal men of the town, of which the foreman was Dr. Jens Skelderup, Bishop of Bergen. (Gaedeke, 396.) By them he was fully acquitted of the charge of "piracy," with which his enemies had and have so consistently and falsely branded him. There is not the slightest basis for such a charge. This was about 2d September, 1567. After this, the Governor of Bergen Castle showed Bothwell great honor, and gave him a magnificent banquet. The Earl always mentions this governor with favor, and styles him "that good lord Erik Rosenkrands." Nevertheless, however courteously treated, Bothwell was, in fact, a prisoner, and when Captain Aalborg sailed from Bergen, 30th September, for Copenhagen, he carried Bothwell and some of his people with him. In the author's "Vindication" of Bothwell, he has furnished the dry details of the Earl's detention in Denmark, of which the following is the summary: The king, Frederic II., would not consent to the extradition of Bothwell at the urgent requests either of the usurping Scottish government or of Queen Elizabeth, nor would he let him go free. Comparing lesser things with grander, it was exactly the case of "The great Apostle" and the Roman Governor—"and Felix, willing to show the Jews a pleasure, left Paul bound." Frederic II. and Bothwell never met, but corresponded. In a letter, dated 18th November, 1567, the King designated Bothwell as "Our particular Favorite," and the Earl is syled in the correspondence, "the Scottish King," On receiving Bothwell's statement, Frederic allowed him to remain at Copenhagen, supplying him with apparel suitable to his rank and liberal entertainment.

In January, 1568, when the pressure of the Scotch regency became stronger, Bothwell was transferred to Malmo Castle*—then in Denmark, now in Sweden—on the

---

* "MALMO.—Soon church-towers arise in the distance, shipping, and a harbor; to the right stands a grim old castle, with staircase—gable and high-pitched roof, encircled by moat and bastion—once the prison of Scotland's proudest earl, the bad and reckless Bothwell. [See engraving, Malmo-huus, page 216.]

"An ancient plan of Malmöhus is preserved in the archives of the Radhus, by refering to which we discover the '*corps de logis*' to be the original palace of King Frederik II.'s time; the remaining buildings were added by Christian IV., as is testified by his cypher, entwined with that of his queen, Anna Catherine, A. K. 1608. * *
But, before searching out his prison, we must first turn to the story of Bothwell himself, according to the records (some sixty-eight in number) which still exist in the Royal Archives of Copenhagen. In the autumn of the year, 1567, Bothwell arrived at Copenhagen, where we find him, about the latter end of December, a prisoner in the *king's palace*.

"Frederik was at that time absent from the capital, hunting at Frederiksborg, from whence he issued the following order to Biörn Kaas, the Seneschal of Malmö :

"Frederik, &c. Be it known to you that we have ordered our wellbeloved Peter Oxe, our man, councillor and marshal of the kingdom of Denmark, to send the Scottish earl, who resides in the castle of Copenhagen, over to our castle of Malmö, where he is to remain for some

northern shore of the Sound, about opposite Copenhagen. As the greater part of this castle was subsequently destroyed by fire, or "submerged in the stormy waves,"

---

time. We request of you, therefore, to have prepared that same vaulted room in the castle where the Marshal, Eyler Hardenberg, had his apartment, and to cover over with mason-work the private place in the same chamber; and, where the iron bars of the windows may not be sufficiently strong and well guarded, that you will have them repaired; and when he arrives, that you will put him into the said chamber, give him beds and *good entertainment*, as Peter Oxe will further direct and advise you; and that you will, above all things, keep a strong guard, and hold in good security the said earl, as you may best devise, that he may not escape. Such is our will.

"Written at Frederiksborg, 28th December, 1567."   *   *

"We entered the square court of the castle, and * * inquired whether there still existed any 'vaulted rooms' in the building of King Frederik II. time. In reply, we were informed that there were two large vaulted chambers on the ground floor, to one of which was attached a small square cabinet, scooped out in the thickness of the castle wall, towards the moat side. An exterior flight of steps led us to the entry of the chamber in which there is every reason to suppose that Bothwell passed some five years—may be the most tranquil of his unquiet life. It is a lofty, oblong, vaulted room, some thirty feet in length, lighted by strongly-barred windows looking on the court. On opening the door of the square closet, the floor was still covered over with mason-work of a blackish stone, well-worn, and polished by the friction of ages—that long narrow pavement so generally used in buildings of the sixteenth century. We quitted the castle perfectly satisfied that we had found the 'vaulted chamber' we had come in search of—the state-room of early days, in which the husband of Scotland's queen, Frederik II.'s own kinswoman, was ordered to receive '*good treatment*.' On the head of Bothwell, as on that of Mary, rested a fearful accusation—that of murder—an accusation which Frederik II. was reluctant to credit, as he writes word in his letter to the infant James, then eighteen months old, in answer to an epistle penned by the hand

there is no certainty as to what portion was assigned as an abode for "the most distinguished state prisoner of Frederic II." It is supposed that he was located in a

---

of Murray. The Danish sovereign refused to receive Bothwell into his presence; but, though he ordered him to be kept *a prisoner, he wished him to enjoy all the comforts and luxuries due to his rank and position*, EVERYTHING SAVE LIBERTY, 'until his case could have better consideration.' Of the doings of Bothwell during his residence at Malmòhus, we know but little. Two days after his arrival (30th December, 1567 [10th January, 1568?]) Peter Oxe writes from Copenhagen to the king to say that the Scottish earl desires to obtain a loan of 200 specie (£40), and to ask whether or not he shall advance it on the king's account; and later, in a MS. register of expenses in the Royal Archives, is preserved a statement, dated 2d March, A.D. 1569, which runs as follows: 'Likewise delivered to Bion Kaas, our man, councillor, and seneschal, at our castle of Malmo; according to order from our high steward aforesaid, English velvet and silk for 75 sp. 6 sk. (£15), of which we have made a present to the Scottish earl, who is imprisoned there.' It was during his imprisonment in Malmòhus that Bothwell composed that narrative of the leading events which terminated in his flight from Scotland, in 1567, as well as of his subsequent adventures, known by the title of 'Les Affaires du Comte de Boduel,' forwarded by him to the Danish sovereign. The MS., entitled 'Les Affaires du Comte de Boduel,' now in the library of Stockholm, is a copy of the original in the handwriting of Dantzay, followed up by his own correspondence with the French king. Bothwell concludes his narrative in the following words: 'Cet ecrit une je prye estre delivré à sa Majesté a fin qu'elle congnosse l'intention et finale volouté de la Royne Madame Marie qui estoit tellelment que je deborois demander a la Majesté de Dannemarch comme allie et confederé de ladite Royne ayde faveur et adsistance tant de geus de guerre que de navires pour la delivrer de la captivité ou elle est.' Lucky had it been for Frederik II. had Bothwell never set his foot on Danish ground, for never was potentate more tormented. First came monthly demands: vehement, and later even violent, from the Earl of Murray, for the handing over of

spacious apartment previously assigned to the governor—a large, oblong, vaulted hall, with windows to the south looking out upon the grand panorama of the Sound, re-

---

the earl's person to his custody for capital punishment, *with even hints of a little previous wholesome torture,* such as boot, maiden, or something worse. Our Virgin Queen, too, dictated four letters on the subject to the Danish King, written in a pretty Italian hand, supposed to be that of Ascham, to not one of which did Frederik (wise man) deign a reply, at which neglect Elizabeth expressed herself much wounded, though in one of them, by way of a sop, she adds with her own royal pen, " Vestra bona soror et consanguinea." But *she got no Bothwell* all the same. Then Catherine de Medicis was sure to write, at least once a month, to her envoy, Charles de Dantzay, 'to insist that Bothwell should *not* be given over to the Scotch.' As to Frederik himself, worried out of his senses, he was not at all inclined to deliver up his prisoner, and that for certain reasons of his own ; for Bothwell, in a letter dated 13th January (1568), had offered, if the king would procure 'la deliverance de Madame Marie la Reyne sa Princesse,' to cede to him the Orkney and Shetland Isles, a regretted appanage, long since severed from the Danish crown.*

"As matters stood, therefore, it was perhaps as well to bear the worry, and see what might turn up later. So he unburdens his mind by writing to the German princes, his relations, explaining to them what he has done, why he has so acted, and asking their advice ; albeit, at the same time determined to follow his own inclination, whatever their answer might be. In the meantime Bothwell goes on drinking, carousing and receiving the visits of his Scotch friends, *snapping his fingers at Queen Elizabeth and the Scottish peers*, until the 16th of June (1578), when he is suddenly removed to the castle of Draxholm, in the

---

* " Pour les frais qui y pourroyent estre faicts que je fisse offre à ladite Majesté de vandre les Isles d'Orquenay et de Schetland libres et quittes sans aucune empeschement à la couronne de Dannemarch et de Norwegue comme ils avoyent cydevant quelque tems esté.

"Presenté à Helsingbourg au S. Peter Oxe et S. Jehan Fris Chancellier, le 16th Janvier, 1568."

motely to the west on the Island Hven, the residence of Tycho Brahe; nearer, on the Island of Salthom opposite, and Amager beyond, in fact, the whole interesting and

island of Zealand. On the 28th of June following, Dantzay writes to his master, the King of France: 'Le Roy de Danemarck avoit iusques à pñt assez bien entretenu le Conte Baudouel, mais depuis peu de jours il l'a faut mettre en une fort maulvaise et estroite prison.' In addition to the testimony of Dantzay, the following entry has been lately discovered in a MS. of Karem Brahe, preserved in the library of Odense: 'In the year 1573, on the 16th of June, was the Scottish earl placed at Draxholm.' Scarce had the prisoner been removed when, on the 26th day of the same month, arrives a letter from the new Regent, Morton, demanding the deliverance of 'Damnatæ memoriæ parricidam nostram,' as he terms Bothwell, which, considering he had been himself a party to the murder of Darnley, is strong language, and with this epistle terminates the correspondence, for on the 24th of November following, Dantzay, after first announcing 'Au Roy—Sr Peter Oxe mourut le 24 jour d'Octobre,' continues, 'le Comte de Baudouel, Ecossais, est aussi decedé,' and this report of the Earl's death was believed by Mary herself, and generally credited throughout the whole of Europe, at the very time he was languishing in a damp unwholesome prison (?) of the Castle of Draxholm. It may be inferred that Frederik had been persuaded by his new Minister, Walkendorf, a man not over-scrupulous as to truth, to announce the death of his illustrious prisoner as the best answer to all the reiterated demands for his person, and thus putting an end to the vexed affair for ever. From this date we hear no more of the Earl, until the record of his death on the 14th April, 1578 (?), and his subsequent interment in the church of Faarveile. * * What was the cause of this sudden change in the treatment of the Scottish earl, so well entertained by the King of Denmark for the space of five years? The Protestants, and those who were hostile to Queen Mary's cause, will tell you that from the year 1572, after the massacre of St. Bartholomew, the feelings of the Lutheran ruler of the realm underwent a change towards his Roman Catholic kinswoman, and that Bothwell to him was naught save the husband of Mary. The Roman

lively environs of the Danish capital not farther distant than from ten to twenty miles. Meanwhile the King took care that his food and clothes should be rich and ample. "He

Catholics on their side assert, and that strenuously, the story of his confession to be true, in which he 'malade à l'extremite au chateau de Malmay, declared la Royne innocente de la ditte mort—lui seul ses parens et quelque noblesse autours d'icelle.' The confession of Bothwell, printed by Drummond of Hawthornden, 1625, has disappeared, as well as the other copies known to have existed formerly(?). The Danish archives lend no aid to the solution of the mystery. Frederik may have forwarded the original to Queen Elizabeth, the paper she 'kept quiet,' but *up to the present time the proofs are wanting, and all is doubt and obscurity.* How Malcolm Laing can assert these names are apparently fictitious is surprising. In olden times Malmö, before orthography was settled, was written Malmoye, Malmöge as well as Malmay ; all these terminations being different dialects of the word *o* or *ey* island Malm, sand (Moeso-Gothic)—*ay* (island) being the real signification of the name. The Skane nobles were men of note and position, possessors of the lands and castles alluded to, lansmen and governors of fortresses and districts. The spelling of their names in Queen Mary's letter differs from that of the documents preserved in the Scottish College at Paris, but this is not to be wondered at. I myself, in the 19th century, after two years' familiarity with the Danish language, should be sadly at a loss to write them down correctly from dictation. Though old Otto Brahe, father of the illustrious Tycho, was at that time gathered to his ancestors, yet the province of Skane was peopled by his descendants. But argue as you may—well or ill—until the missing document be forthcoming all will be vexation of spirit—so let the matter rest, and each man hold to his own opinion.

"There is nothing more to relate, so let us bid adieu to the vaulted chamber in the degraded fortress of old Malmo-huus, once a prison, far too good and spacious for the most restless adventurer of his age, the husband of Queen Mary—James Erle Boithuille."—"One Year in Sweden," Vol. I., pages 3-20, by Horace Marryat. From the de Peyster Collection, in the New York Society Library.

was detained there [Malmo] as a State prisoner, indeed, but led a luxurious life, and was treated far better than he deserved, being allowed the liberty of shooting and other recreations, while the King of Denmark ordered and paid for velvet dresses and other costly array for his use." When those "Titans of fraud" and crime, the Scottish authorities, empowered Colonel (*Obrist* or *Oberst*) and Captain John Clark, a Scottish mercenary—nominally commanding, in 1564, 206 Scottish cavalry soldiers in the service of Denmark—to demand the extradition of Bothwell, Bothwell turned the tables upon Clark by showing that when the Danish government sent Clark over to Scotland, in 1567, to enlist troops for its service, this agent was induced to expend the money entrusted to him for that special purpose for the benefit of the "Bonded" Lords in rebellion against Queen Mary and Bothwell, and actually marshalled the soldiers, mustered in to serve Frederic, to fight against the Queen at Carberry Hill. Clark was sent before a court-martial, and, in spite of the remonstrances of Elizabeth and Murray, was found guilty, consigned to the same castle, Dragsholm, that eventually received Bothwell within its dragon ward, and died there, a prisoner, before his intended victim.

After this affair of Clark (1568-70), Frederic II. relaxed the restraint on the Earl, and he was allowed full liberty within the precincts of the castle; nay more, he "was allowed no small liberty in Malmo," dressing in velvet and silk, and leading a tranquil, and by no means an unhappy life. In fact, except that he was not free (Wiesener, 505), "his life was that of a brilliant lord;" an existence far happier, perhaps, and certainly more comfortable than that of the majority of potentates at this era. At a later date, it is said, Captain Clark became reconciled with Bothwell in Dragsholm, and together they drowned their cares and ennui in wine. This kind of living killed Clark in July, 1575, and seriously injured the health of Bothwell.

Dissolution.

All upon a summer sea
Sailing in an argosy—
　Rebecs, lutes and viols sounding,
　While the ship o'er wavelets bounding,
Skims the surface of the sea.
　＊　＊　＊　＊　＊
Stealing down a gloomy river,
Where dull water-grasses quiver,
　From a barque come sounds of sorrow,
　Never ceasing with the morrow—
Mournful barque upon the river.
　＊　＊　＊　＊　＊
Sullen clouds obscure the moon,
Darkness cometh all too soon!
　Black the clouds and black the river,
　Black the barque, and oh! the shiver
As it sinks beneath the moon!—*The Argosy.*

ACT V. SCENE LAST. (ABBREVIATED.)

[CARBERRY HILL. A knoll, whence the prospect extends to the westward and northward, looking over the nearer lines of the Queen's forces, and towards those, beyond, of the Confederate Lords. In the immediate rear stand three pieces of artillery, pointed at the latter, with a few "Constables" in charge: of whom one, assigned to each gun, at intervals waves his linstock to keep the slow-match alight and ready for immediate use. Near these are groups of royal regular Hackbutteers, belonging to the Queen's body-guard, at ease, and parties of Border noblemen and their retainers, Jackmen, evidently as if just dismounted, and leaning on their long spears. In the front centre are Mary Stuart and Bothwell; and, to the right, but withdrawn a space, Kirkaldy of Grange. Behind the Queen is Captain Blackadder, one of Bothwell's subordinates, watching what is occurring in the enemy's ranks, and his remarks serve as an explanation or *Chorus.*]

BLACKADDER. [*To Bothwell.*]
Hasten, my Lord, your colloquy: the foe
Are striving to outflank us. Look, their horse
To close the road to Dunbar, headlong spur.
If fight 's the word, now is the time to fight,
Lest we both lose advantage of the sun
Full in their faces; our position too;
And worst, if beaten, our retreat 's cut off.

MARY. [Continuing a conversation which had been going
on before the scene opened.]
I am resolv'd to trust Kirkaldy—
BOTHWELL. Ah!
What glamour blinds thee, love? Thou know'st him not:
The hireling spy and England's traitrous tool.
He but deceives thee, with his specious tale;
His boasted chivalry is mere lacker.
Beneath the semblance of the golden truth
Is falsehood's foul and cheap-jack metal. Think
Ere you commit your fortune to such crew.
[Bothwell breaks off suddenly, rushes to a Hackbutteer and, by signs and words inaudible
to the spectators, directs him to shoot Kirkaldy, who, shading his eyes against the
declining sun, is looking in a different direction towards his own friends. Mary,
moved by Bothwell's charges, seems lost for a moment in deep thought; then suddenly
perceives Bothwell's intention and throws herself between the musketeer and his aim.]

MARY. What would'st thou do?
BOTHWELL, Slay the deceiving villain
By whom you are infatuated.
MARY. James,
He 's under safeguard of my queenly word,
And, though he were the very knave thou say'st,
He must not die by an assassin shot.
BOTHWELL. [With difficulty restraining himself, and
making a gesture to the musketeer to " recover
arms," returns to the Queen's side.]
My love, my queen, my sweetheart and my life,
Thy noble nature and thy native sense
Are both the victims of this knave's device.
Is it not better, here upon this field,
To strike one blow for honor and thy crown
Than thus abase thyself to traitors—yield
Thy freedom, and perchance thy life, to those
Who never yet have kept a single Bond
Beyond the signing, had their purposes
But borne their fruit perfidious. Hast thou not
Prov'd me, as never yet woman prov'd man
Or had the chance to do 't? Have I not shown,
By ev'ry thought, word, act, since manhood's dawn,
That Truth and Bothwell were synonymous?
" KIIP TREST!" my motto—emblem of my life.
Was I not faithful to my mother; then
With equal truth did I not turn to thee:
Until thy love, enkindled at my own,
Or my big love, inflam'd by thy bright eyes,
Converted me from loyalty to love?
Have I e'er fail'd thee? Have I not been truth,
Love, faith, devotion: *all* thy sex can ask?
And yet thou dost not trust me; but prefer'st
The specious promise of a hireling tongue!
MARY. I am resolv'd to trust the Bonded Lords;
Not, that I have lost faith in thee, mine own,
But cause 't would seem as if by Fate impell'd,
This is the wisest course and fits the time.
A brief, sad parting and a better meeting
May bring again a long and halcyon term.

BOTHWELL. No, no! No, no! I tell thee, No! 'T would seem
As if, on board a stout still lusty frigate,
Because 't is slightly shatter'd by a squall,
Thou would'st abandon ship and practic'd captain,
To trust a pirate's skiff to save from storm
That lowers, but has not burst. Oh! Mary,
Dost thou love me?
  MARY. My acts are the best answer
I have gone through too much for thee to doubt it.
Oh, what have I not done to prove my love? [*Wringing her hands.*]
Oh, what have I not suffer'd to be thine?
  BOTHWELL. Then, by the tie united us when twain,
And by the two church rites that made us one,
I do conjure thee, let me fight this day:
Not like a felon bid me steal away,
Never before has Bothwell quit the field,
But all victorious or upon his shield.

[Bothwell takes Mary's hand in his, and they stand thus, grasping each others hands, for some minutes; then clasp each other in a sad but fierce embrace. He glues his lips to hers, then suddenly releases her, and, gazing, seems to discern that neither kisses nor caresses have changed her resolution. His eyes question her.]

  MARY. [*Suddenly.*] I am resolv'd to keep my word to Grange.
  BOTHWELL. Oh, love! my life!
  MARY. [*With a sad smile.*] Alas! we here must part;
Part for a time, assur'd of future meeting.
  BOTHWELL. Wilt thou be true to me, and keep thy promise,
So often seal'd with kisses, e'en beside
The dead man's corse; to ne'er even in thought,
Nor word, nor bond, nor deed, annul nor weaken it;
Be my own Mary, till the whelming sea
Or the cold earth put seal to either life?
  MARY. I promise. Go! Before it is too late,
Take horse for Dunbar, ere the foeman's horse
Cut in and make escape impossible.
  BOTHWELL. [*With desperation.*] Will you not fight,
      or let us fight?
  MARY.   Too late!

[Bothwell seizes her in his arms and kisses her wildly; but, seeing that even in this supreme moment she makes a motion for Kirkaldy to approach, he suddenly releases her and strides to the left of the stage; then turns, and perceives that Kirkaldy has drawn nearer to the Queen. Some one in the rear has given a signal to the enemy, and without, to the right, arise shouts, fanfares of trumpets and triumphant flams of drums.]

  BOTHWELL. [*To those without.*] Ho! To horse! To horse!
  MARY. [*Giving her hand to Kirkaldy.*] Come, Sir, let us go!

These two last exclamations are simultaneous as the curtain falls. Rude, loud, triumphant music accompanies its descent, which gradually changes into softer and mournful notes, as the curtain again rises upon a double scene.]

FOTHERINGAY.	DRAGSHOLM.
Mary, with her head on the block, and the executioner standing over her with upraised axe.	Bothwell, lying dead upon the floor of his dungeon at Adelsborg.

[Curtain falls again to sad music, which gradually changes into a symphony, as it rises on the reunion of Mary and Bothwell.]

"JAMES HEPBURN, Earl of Bothwell," *an unpublished Tragedy.*

JUNE 16th, 1573, why does not appear, Bothwell was privately transferred to the Castle of Dragsholm* (Dragon's Island), now Adelsborg. Dragsholm appears to be an isthmus (island?) between Seiro Bay and the La(o)mme Fiorde, one of the arms of the Ise-Fiorde, on the northwest coast of Zealand, fifty-eight miles west of Copenhagen, off the road between the seaport towns of Holbek,

---

* Leaving the highroad from Copenhagen to Holbek, "before long the imposing Chateau of [Dragsholm, now] Adelsborg [the last place of confinement for Bothwell] appeared in sight, well placed among the surrounding woods, * * * in a private demesne. * * * As we approach the borders of the [tranquil] fiorde, on a little promontory jutting out into the sea, stands a whitewashed gabled church, and its spire of ancient date, simple and unadorned, but made to paint, the village Church of Faareveile, within whose walls repose [what are erroneously represented as] the mortal remains of the Earl of Bothwell, the so-called [the third and best beloved] husband of Mary Stuart, who died a prisoner, some say a maniac, within the walls of Draxholm, where he had been privately removed by the King of Denmark. * * The ancient castle of DRAXHOLM, or *Dragon's Island*, was, in former days, the property of the Bishop of Roeskilde; the huge mass of buildings are still something ecclesiastical in their appearance, surrounded by a moat, and of no architectural beauty. The great tower [represented] in the old engravings of Resen, was destroyed by the Swedes, in 1658; the chapel gutted during the War of the Counts, in 1533. It is the intention of [the present owner, 1860,] Baron Zeutphen Adeler to restore [it] to its former state. * * Before we proceed to visit the church of Faareveile, I may as well explain [in my way] how Bothwell came to end his days within the prison of the castle of Draxholm.

"It was in the year 1567 that sentence of death was passed by the Scottish Parliament on the Earl of Bothwell, at that time resident in

to the east, and Kallundsborg, to the west. Faareveile, where the body of Bothwell is said to have been deposited, is on, or near by, the shore of the L(a)omme Fiorde.

---

the Orkney Islands, having under his command a squadron of five light-armed vessels of war, * * * Bothwell's squadron, endeavoring, during a terrific storm, to escape from an armament sent in their pursuit [all mixed up, truth and error], two of his vessels managed to enter the harbor of Karmsund, in Norway. Bothwell here declared himself to be the husband of the Queen of Scots, and demanded to be conducted into the presence of the King of Denmark. Such is the account given by English historians. Now, however, that Bothwell is safe arrived in Norway, it is as well to consult the account given by the Danes themselves. In the '*Liber Bergensis Capituli*' we find the following notice :

· "'September 2, A.D. 1568 [1567], came the King's ship "David," upon which Christian of Aalborg was head man: she had taken prisoner a Count [Earl] from Scotland, of the name of JACOB HEBROE *of Botwile*, who first was made Duke of the Orkneys and Shetland, and lately married the Queen of Scotland, and after he was suspected of having been in the counsel to blow up the King [Darnley]: they first accused the Queen, and then the Count, but he made his escape, and came to Norway, and was afterwards taken to Denmark by the king's ship "David [Bear]."' *The accusation of piracy made against the Scottish earl was never credited by Frederic II., or his advisers.* Bothwell had hired two [two-masted, lesser war-ships, called] pinks, when in Shetland, of Gerhard Hemlin the Bremois, for fifty silver dollars a month, commanded by David Wodt, a noted pirate [privateer, or letter of marque, for the terms were then synonymous and expressed by the same word], in which he arrived on the coast of Norway, in a miserable plight, his own vessel [flag ship] having returned to Shetland, with his valuables on board, to fetch his people [and valuables]. Erik Rosenkrantz, the Governor [of Bergen], thought necessary to summon a jury of the most respectable people of the town, 'twelve brewers of the bridge,' to enquire into the Earl's case, and how it was he had become associated with so well-known a pirate. Some of the crew affirmed they knew of

According to generally received accounts, Bothwell was plunged into a dungeon. This is mere surmise. Nothing is positively known.

no other captain than one Wodt, to whom the pink belonged. The commission add, that this Hamburger (as Bothwell styles him in his narrative) was a well-known pirate.

"Still they suspected the Earl was about to go over to Sweden, a country at war with Denmark; they accordingly recommend that he should take an oath that he would keep peace towards his Danish Majesty's subjects, as well as towards all those who brought goods to his Majesty's dominions. On this account only [a fear that the Earl was about to serve the Swedes, and not for piracy] Erik Rosenkrantz sends him a prisoner to Copenhagen. This was, no doubt, the origin of the accusation of 'piracy' made by the Earl of Murray [an unrelenting, malignant, personal foe] against Bothwell by the mouth of the infant king [James VI.], aged eighteen months. *The Earl had come to raise men in the North to aid the royal* [Mary's and his own] *cause*. Indeed, so satisfactory was his examination on this point, it is mentioned in the '*Liber Bergensis*' that, two days after his examination—

"September 28th [1567], Erik Rosenkrantz gave to the Earl and his noblemen a magnificent banquet; and, again, 'the Earl repaired to the Castle, and Erik received him with great honor.' * * * *

"On the 30th September, comes our last notice: 'The Earl was conducted to a ship and led prisoner to Denmark, that is Malmo-huus. This assertion is not quite correct; as Bothwell remained in Copenhagen until the 30th of December [until 10th January, 1568, if not later], when he was consigned to the custody of Biorn Kaas, Governor of Malmo-huus, together with his companion, Captain Clarke. *Here he remained, well treated, with a liberal allowance from the King of Denmark*, indulging in potations with his comrade, which later brought him to death's door. Many were the requests from the Queen of England and the Scottish Lords to Frederick, demanding that the Earl should be handed over to their custody, to which the Danish Sovereign always replied by a refusal. If they chose to proceed against him they were are at liberty so to do, but judged he must be by Danish

Even Agnes Strickland is forced to admit that the popular tradition of Bothwell's madness is entirely without foundation, and that when at Dragsholm he was treated much

laws. It is related how, after a season, being brought to a state of weakness from the effects of a dangerous illness, his conscience tormented by anguish and remorse [utterly false], he made, in the presence of several witnesses, a confession of his share of Darnley's assassination, exonerating Queen Mary from any participation or knowledge of his crime. Mary, in a letter to her Ambassador on the subject, writes the names of those before whom the attestation was made, to be: Otto Braw, of the Castle of Elcembre; Paris Braw, of Vascu; Monsieur Gullensterna, of the Castle of Fulkenster; Baron Cowes, of Malinga Castle; so Miss Strickland gives them. I have this morning consulted a Danish *nobilier* to see whether I can, among the manors once in possession of these families, find any names similar to those here given. The spelling is obscure, but really not worse than that of a foreigner of the 19th century, if he attempted to write down the names by ear.

"Otto Braw, of the Castle of Elcembre, stands for Otto Brahe, of the Castle of Helsingborg, of which he was governor—father of Tycho Brahe. He died, however, in 1571. [It does not stand to reason that a corse was admitted as a subscribing witness, except in a blood-and-thunder drama, such as the Old Bowery 'Dead Hand.'] His son, Steen, was at that time alive, and resided near Malmo—indeed, the whole province of Skaane teemed with his family, *lehnsmend* and governors, high in authority. Paris Braw, of Vascu, I take to be Brahe, of Vidskovle, a chateau near Christianstad; Gullensterna of Fulkenster, Gyldenstierne of Fuletofte, probably Axel, son of Mogens Gyldenstierne, Stadtholder of Malmo, and himself a Governor; while for Baron Cowes, of Malinge, read Biorn Kaas, Governor of Malmo-huus, whose son, Jorgen, was possessor of Meilgard, in Jutland.

"In the copy of Bothwell's confession, preserved in the Scotch College in Paris, these names are again differently written. The Swedes, to whom Skaane now belongs, possess again an orthography different

better than he deserved; perhaps not worse than Mary was by Elizabeth. Schiern has demonstrated with greater clearness the *utter falsity* of the CONFESSION attributed to

---

from the Danes. You will not find them written in two books alike. After a lapse of fifty years, nothing can be more puzzling.

" It was in the year 1573, after the confession, that Bothwell was removed to Draxholm, and treated as a criminal; *though of that no documentary evidence exists.* * * * M. de Dantzay [The French ambassador] writes word to Charles IX. that the King of Denmark, up to the present time, had well treated the Earl of Bothwell, but a few days since had caused him to be put ' en une fort maulvaise et estroite prison.' [This may simply refer to the strength of the Dragon Island keep and its loneliness, characteristics which would affect the judgment and language of a Frenchman accustomed to court life and long residence in a refined capital.] In the month of November, the same year [1573], he again announces, ' le Comte de Baudouel, Ecossais, est aussi décédé.' Bothwell, however, did not die till April 19th, 1578. [Not so, 1575 :—1578 is disproved by the very narrator further on.] According to the chaplain of Draxholm, Frederic, tormented by the demands of Queen Elizabeth and the Scotch Regents for his deliverance into their hands, *allowed the report of his death to be circulated, and so put an end to all the worry on the subject.*

" In the chronicle of Frederic II.'s reign, Resen, under the year 1578, after stating that Frederic II. caused the dead body of his father to be removed from Odense to Rosiklde, continues : ' At that very time the Scottish Earl Bothwell also died, after a long imprisonment at Draxholm, and was buried at Faareveile.' That the Scottish Queen, in her damp prison of Fotheringay, receiving her intelligence in secret, should have been misinformed as to the christian names of the Danish noblemen who were summoned to the sick-bed of Bothwell, is not surprising ;—such a confusion, too, as exists in these ancient geneologies ; such an intermarrying between the families of Kaas, Gyldenstierne, and Brahe ; such a changing and exchanging of manors by sale, by dowry, by gifte, *maal and morgen gaffue* (marriage settlement)—my head,

Bothwell. In all the authentic papers known to have been written by him, he insists upon his innocence, and with equal force alleges the guilt of Murray and Morton, and

before we had finished our researches, became a very chaos. [It was, the story shows it.]

"The [supposed] prison of Bothwell is now the wine-cellar of the castle, and the iron ring, to which he is reported to have been attached a maniac [which is false], stands inserted in the wall, between two shelves of the wine-bins—on one lies crusty Port, in the lower Chateau Lafitte. What a tantalizing sight for his wine-loving spectre, should he by chance revisit the seat of his former prison! *Bothwell died at Draxholm two years after his removal thither* [1573, consequently 1575, *not* 1578], and was interred in the parish church of Faareveile. * * * On the iron-bound door [of the church] appears the dragon, titular patron, I suppose, of the place. The interior is simple, of good architecture, with pulpit and altar-piece of Christian IV.'s date, and in sound repair. * * * They raise a folding trap [since definitely closed] in the chancel; a ladder leads to the vault below; on the right lies a simple wooden coffin, encased in an outer one for protection: the lid is removed, a sheet withdrawn, uncovered within which lies the mummy-corpse [this is altogether without proof and apocryphal] of Scotland's proudest Earl. The coffin in earlier times reposed in a vault of the chapel of the Adeler family, but was removed by the baron to its present place for the convenience of those who desire to visit it without intruding on the dormitory of the family. It had always, for centuries, been known as the tomb of 'Grev. Bodvell" by sacristan and peasant. When the wooden coffin was first opened, the body was found enveloped in the finest linen, the head reposing on a pillow of satin (?) THERE WAS NO INSCRIPTION.

Now, I am no enthusiast, and take matters quietly enough, but I defy any impartial *Englishman* [a nationality most inimical to Bothwell living and dead] to gaze on this body without at once declaring it to be that of an ugly Scotchman. [? ! ? ! ? ! Ridiculous assertion, and no proof whatever, as Schiern demonstrates.] It is that of a man about the middle height—and to judge by his hair, red mixed with

their associates. Even at Draxholm, it is stated that Bothwell "nevertheless, got permission to go hunting." It is supposed that Frederic transferred the Earl from Malmo to Dragsholm to relieve himself from the annoyances of the applications made by the successive Regents of Scotland and the Queen of England. In her endeavors to injure Bothwell with Frederic II. and retaliate upon the Earl in his distress for his life-long patriotic refusals of her invitations to imitate Murray, Morton, Kirkaldy and others, and become her tool, spy, and, like Murray, her "fawning spaniel," traitor to his country, she descended to the meanness of styling Darnley as "King," whereas she had hitherto refused him that title, both while living and when dead,

---

grey, of about fifty years of age. The forehead is not expansive; the form of the head wide behind, denoting bad qualities, of which Bothwell, as we all know [how, by misrepresentation? yes!] possessed plenty; high cheek-bones; remarkably prominent, long, hooked nose, somewhat depressed towards the end (this may have been the effect of emaciation); wide mouth; *hands and feet small, well shaped, those of a high-bred man.* I have examined the records of the Scottish Parliament, caused researches to be made at the British Museum—the copy of his 'Hue and Cry' is not forthcoming; *no description of Bothwell exists* [great error], save that of Brantome, who saw [is supposed to have seen] him on his visit to Paris, where he first met Mary, during the lifetime of King Francis. * * Having first severed a lock of his red and silver hair as a souvenir, we let close the coffin-lid. * * Bothwell's life was a troubled one; but, had he selected a site in all Christendom for quiet and repose in death, he could have found none more peaceful, more soft and calm, than the village church of Faarveile." (HORACE MARRYATT's "Jutland and the Danish Isles;" pp. 408-19. de Peyster Alcove, N. Y. Society Library.)

styling him in her correspondence "the dead gentleman," "*le mort gentilhomme*" (Buckingham, I., 363–'4). Now she invoked vengeance upon Bothwell, as the cruel assassin of his relative and sovereign. And here it may be pertinent to observe that Bothwell was of the noblest blue blood on all sides. He was as nearly related to Mary as he was to his divorced wife, Jane Huntley, as he was descended from Joanna, daughter of James I., King of Scotland, and also from Queen Joanna, or Jane Beaufort, wife of James I., by her second husband, Sir James Stewart, "the Black Knight of Lorn." That Bothwell was in any degree related to Darnley is not shown.

When and where did Bothwell die? Many say in Malmo-huus. Sheer ignorance! Shiern says 14th April,

Malmo-huus.

1578; Petrick in the beginning of November, 1575. Whether he died in 1575 or 1578 there is nothing positive known of the details of his life after 1571.*

Reader, have you ever met with "Historic Doubts,"

---

* He made no Confession, he left no Testament inculpating himself or exonerating Mary in connection with the Darnley killing, and everything of the kind attributed to him are manipulations or forgeries. The best authorities now unite in conceding this. "Mary Stuart received the intelligence of Bothwell's decease"—says Gaedeke, 410—"without being much moved at it; passionate natures like hers have ever been wanting in feeling." Just so! She was a heartless, although excitable woman. Now Bothwell, then Darnley; now Bothwell then Norfolk, and then the Axe. Anathema upon her, she was unworthy of a "REAL MAN."

Schiern, Petrick and others have shown that no amount of research can discover any data to enable the biographer or antiquarian to lift even the lowest corner of the veil of doubt and ignorance which hangs over the last years of Bothwell. Schiern (386) corroborates Petrick. "The Earl's coffin was brought from Dragsholm to the nearest church at Faareveile. This church, which stands away from the village, on the west bay of Isefjord, in a lonely and quiet spot, the haunt of gulls and sea-fowl, is said to be the last resting-place of him who was the third and best loved husband of Scotland's Queen.

"As tradition still points out in Dragsholm the room which was Bothwell's prison, so among the coffins in Faareveile church, it continues to indicate one, without any inscription or adornment, as the coffin of the famous Scotsman. To ascertain the truth of the legend, the coffin was opened on the 31st of May, 1858, but without any positive mark being seen that the corpse found in it was really Bothwell's."

Marryat asserts that, unmistakably, the body he saw was that of an ugly Scotchman. Schiern explodes such a silly argument and assertion by citing the fact that "Bothwell was not the only Scotchman that was buried in Faareveile Church," and added the question, "How much of the 'ugliness' alleged here ought to be ascribed to the fact of the

or any one of the careful treatises written to prove how unworthy of trust are generally received traditions and the majority of histories, so styled. Do you know? Can you answer at once, Who was Joab? The author has asked this question indiscriminately many hundreds of times, and, except from a constant Bible reader, scarcely ever got a correct answer, if any at all, and yet Joab was the grand and able general of a great king, the father of the wisest monarch that ever grasped a sceptre, and the story of Joab, David and Soloman is told in the Book read by all civilized people. Joab's dispositions and victory at Medeba constitute an example of a class of peculiar battles, of which the latest was our Chancellorsville. Who was Simon Stevin of Bruges? A Dutch mathematician, who was the first to throw light on the darkness which had brooded upon the world, for 1800 years, since Archimedes. Maurice of Nassau was the restorer of military discipline; Simon Stevin was his preceptor in military science, proper,

---

body having passed three hundred years in the grave, it is certainly not so easy to determine." Why was not this the body of Captain Clark? Marryat says that the corpse he saw was that of a man of middle size. This does not agree with the traditional full-length "columnar," "overtopping tall," portrait of Bothwell. The famous Prussian General, von Moltke, justly conceded that great men would not enjoy posthumous excellence and immortality without poets and historians. By impartial pens Bothwell was represented as a stalwart, columnar, martial figure, as a powerful and imposing military chief, whose resounding tread rang battleward.

castrematation and engineering. Who was John Cavalier? A little Protestant baker's boy, in a small town among the mountains of Languedoc, who, at the age of twenty, made an army, equipped with weapons, mostly curiosities preserved in old armories, until he wrested better from his foes. With some three thousand peasants whom he had drilled, he held at bay sixty thousand regulars—veterans, volunteers and militia—and was a match in succession for two Marshals of France, one of whom was the celebrated Villars, who declared that his youthful opponent had performed "actions worthy of Cæsar." He treated as equal with equal with this same Villars, who was a local *Alter Ego* of Louis XIV., and by keeping such a mass of the best French troops in check in southern France, Cavalier converted Marlborough's campaign, which culminated at Blenheim, 13th August, 1704, from a probability into a certainty, that burst at once the bubble of French invincibility. Bothwell belonged to this class of marvels. Henry Taylor, author of the wonderful dramatic poem, "Philip van Artevelde," tells us

"The world knows nothing of its greatest men."

"Such souls,
Whose sudden visitations daze the world,
Vanish like lightning, but they leave behind
A voice that in the distance far away
Wakens the slumbering ages."

Bothwell lived on, and died at Dragsholm (? 1575, '76 or '78) faithful to the motto of his house, "KIIP TREST!"

Dragsholm Castle.

Keep Trust! Be faithful!

"A gentleman of credit, noble, honest,—
As true as his own sword."

His devotion, boy and man, to Mary of Guise, Queen-Dowager and Regent of Scotland, was inviolate and inviolable, and when Queen Mary returned to Edinburgh she still found his loyalty so lofty and unchangeable, that "it seemed to partake of that devotion which shed a halo over the days of Chivalry." Bothwell committed the crime which, in this world, never receives any other than the enigmatic absolution accorded by Pope Pius III. to the

murderers of Cardinal Beatoun, "REMITTIMUS IRREMISI-
BILE." "*We pardon the deed which admits of no pardon.*" Bothwell's crime—such a deed—was FAILURE, and, despite his loyalty, bravery, ability, patriotism and manifold other gifts,

> "He left a name at which [his] world grew pale
> To point a moral, or adorn a tale."

Bothwell's culmination or transit realized the language of Macbeth, about to perish:

> "Life's but a walking shadow; a poor player,
> That struts and frets his hour upon the stage,
> And then is heard no more: it is a tale
> Told by an idiot full of sound and fury,
> Signifying nothing."

Bothwell's Book-Stamp.

APPENDIX.

ARNOLD GAEDEKE (Giessen, 1879,) on the Authenticity of the Casket ("*Chatoullen*") Letters, &c. Translated from the original German.

The genuineness of these celebrated letters has so often been a subject of the most embittered controversy, and so many hypotheses of all sorts, made with such an expenditure of ability, have been advanced* concerning it, that a rehearsal of all the arguments brought out for and against it, appears superfluous, especially since, to the opponents of their authenticity, little peculiarities and immaterial circumstances count for more than the most obvious deductions. *The genuineness of the letters—in my opinion—if one excepts perfect verbal correctness,† no longer admits of a doubt.* The attempts of the majority of recent writers must, decidedly, be rejected,‡ and the rather should this be done, that as good as nothing new is brought forward by them, as a basis for their views. It is the old *hair-splitting*, as to date, style, &c., which is again raked up, and which we encounter about equally in all of them.

There is only the fierce attack on Crawford's deposition, with the reasons given for it, which is new, and, therefore, of some importance, for this a document lately discovered among the Hamilton Papers has furnished the material. This document is a letter which Darnley's father, the Earl of Lenox, it is said, directed to Crawford from Chiswick. In it he conjures him, for God's sake, to furnish further matter of accusation against the Queen, or else the worst result—that is to say, the acquittal of Mary Stuart—was to be feared at York. "By all possible methods, to search for more matters against her," writes Lenox to Crawford, June 11th, 1568. ("Hamilton Papers;" Hosack, I., 199.) ☞ It is well known that the adherents of Mary Stuart have falsified to an enormous extent, and the circumstance that they should have been found in the possession of the Hamiltons is moreover very striking.

However—granted the genuineness of this letter—we can in the extremest case only conclude from it that Crawford, who had been summoned to York as a witness, and was preparing his testimony before hand, may have obtained previous knowledge of the contents of the *Chatoullen* letters, and the contents of the Lenox letter shows nothing at all against their genuineness. The *Chatoullen* letters had been long before the Scottish Parliament. Besides this the anxiety of Lenox was natural. When he wrote the letter in question, Murray had not yet thrown aside his hesitating attitude, which the Duke of Norfolk evidently had caused him to take, and he held back with the principal article of accusation. The anxiety of Lenox was acutely shared by Queen Elizabeth and by the English Commissioners. It is also to be remembered that Throckmorton had already declared, in a report of 15th July, 1567, that there were in Scotland proofs, in Mary's own handwriting—and finally, it is further to be borne in mind, that

---

* The attempt of Wiesener has been very justly rejected by Maurenbrecher ("historische Zeitschrift," XIV., 521 ff.)

† The original letters and the original casket (Fassung) are no longer to be found. The letters were in the possession first of Morton, then of Gowrie, and, finally, came into the hands of *James VI., who, no doubt, destroyed them.* We have only the Scotch and Latin translation, as also the retranslation into French of 1572.

‡ The opinion of the correspondent of the *Augsburger Allgemeine Zeitung*, of the 5th May, 1878, appears very groundless and rash. In a criticism of the works of Chantelauze and Morris he is bold enough to assert, on the basis of the recent publications, "that the view founded on a shuffle can scarcely any longer enjoy general assent."

the, as yet, cherished idea, that, the falsity of one letter being proved, the fate of all the others is decided, does not answer in historical criticism.

The chief arguments for the genuineness of the *Chatoullen* [difficult to be dealt with?] letters have, up to the present time, been the following:

1. The agreement of the first principal letter with the declarations of Crawford, to whom Darnley, immediately after his interview with the Queen, imparted what was said, in order that the former should give an account of it to his father.

2. The mention of Hiegate, &c., a circumstance which no falsifier could have invented. This Hiegate was a town-clerk of Glasgow, who was said to have made a declaration as to the intention of Darnley to obtain possession of the young prince, his son. The Queen wrote about the affair to Archbishop Beatoun on the 20th January, 1567, and for many years no one knew how to explain the passage concerning it.

3. The peculiar form of the letter, which breaks off in the middle, from want of paper, &c., and is afterwards finished.

4. The confidential letter of the Earl of Lenox to his wife, in which the finding of the *Chatoullen* letters is discussed.

5. The unanimous decision of the English Commissioners, among whom was the Duke of Norfolk. No one held the letters to be falsified, there is nothing of the sort mentioned in the record.

6. The behavior of the Queen herself. Her commissioners declared, only on the 6th December, that all writings which could be brought forward by the rebels were calumnies and private communications, which could in no way be prejudicial to their mistress. Finally the Queen herself declared that Murray was, without doubt, in possession of papers of the highest importance.

To these proofs we are, in my opinion, now able to add a new and not inconsiderable argument. A passage of that first letter has remained up to this day (it has escaped even Froude) unconsidered, and this, simply, because it was not understood. We have, only within a few years, obtained the key to it through Teulet's publications. Just at the commencement of the conversation, we find a short question of Darnley's, whether the Queen had already prepared her "*état*," a question which she answers in the affirmative. We now know that this "*état*" was a List, prepared for inspection, of pensions and pensioners, and which was paid in France, out of the widows's-portion of the Queen, 40,000 Livres ; and that this list was prepared annually and forwarded to France, in order to serve as a *warrant* for the payments. The chief part of the recipients were Frenchmen, or servants living in France, as Beatoun, the ambassador, who received 3,060 Livres. The document of February, 1567, is in existence, signed by Mary Stuart and her secretary, Joseph Rizzio, brother of David, and, therefore, must have been prepared immediately before the Glasgow visit. (Estat des gaiges des dames, desmoiselles, gentilzhommes et outres officiers domestiques de la Royne d'Ecosse, Douairiaire de France. Teulet II., 268.)

It is almost impossible that a falsifier should have hit upon this question, and very unlikely that the fact, in general, was known to many persons. Its being a short simple question is of consequence here ; if a falsifier had wished to make use of the circumstance, the passage would, without doubt, have been worded in an entirely different manner. But it is, most of all, of consequence, that in the Scottish Parliament, when the papers were laid before it, no one stood up for the Queen, although Huntley, Errol, and, above all, Herries were present. A circumstance which alone should be of sufficient weight to confute all the objections of apologists. The Parliament declared that "the process against the Queen was caused by her own offence," which was proved by various confidential letters, in her own hand, written to Bothwell before and after the murder of the King.*

---

* To be attributed to her own default, in so far as be divers her privie lettres written halely by her ann hand, and send be her to James, sometime Earl of Bothwell, chief

I will now turn to the objections which have been made by the other side. As regards the date of the letters, there is to be put into the scale that we have not the original letters, and that, in writing the translations, errors and faults in writing might easily occur. If there were a desire to falsify, it was easy either to omit the date entirely or to give it with the greatest exactness. I can find no contradiction in this regard. The Queen reached Glasgow on the 24th of January; the same night she wrote that long, famous letter to Bothwell, which she finished on the morning of the 25th. Paris set out at once, reached the capital on Saturday night, and brought the answer back to Glasgow on the morning of the 27th. The distances are not so great as to throw any doubt on this. Mary Stuart left Glasgow on the 27th, and arrived at the capital on the 28th. Paris, as a courier, accomplished the journey in still shorter time. Murray's Journal is in error when it makes Bothwell's first arrival in Edinburgh on the 28th, or, what is much more likely, Bothwell, who stayed in the capital on the 25th and 26th, incognito, left the city with Paris, and returned on the 28th.

Hosack's grounds for the spuriousness of the letters have no significance. He directly denies Mary's passion for Bothwell (a thing which cannot be doubted), because she had "known him altogether too long." The audacity of Hosack's conclusions is generally wonderful. He likewise brings up Murray's will as a proof of Mary's innocence.

When Murray, after the murder of Darnley, betook himself to France, he made his will, and in it recommended his only daughter to the care of the Queen, in the most urgent manner. ("Morton Papers." Printed by the Bannetyne Club. I., 19.) At this time Murray had not the slightest knowledge of the *Chatoullen* letters; but, even if he had, he might still have commended his daughter to the care of his sister and sovereign, without thereby admitting the innocence of this last.

The "noisy" method and manner in which Darnley was killed, has also often been brought forward in favor of Mary Stuart. It certainly cannot be denied that the good sense of the Queen would at once cause her, in case she was initiated into the plans *of her lover*, to protest against this way of death, and, if one wishes to be just, it must further be admitted that, besides the declarations of Bothwell's servants—to which I attach but small importance—there is no piece of proof in existence that the Queen had a knowledge of all the details. This, however, diminishes her guilt in a very small degree; it does not even remove the character of treachery from her, since, that something was intended against her husband, Mary Stuart must have known as certainly as it is certain that she stood in a lover's relation with Bothwell. We possess the most indubitable proof of this.

Froude, an opponent, cannot conceal his wonder at the above. A murder by poison, he thinks, would, relatively, have but little injured her character. Aside from the fact that in Scotland such a thing was not usual, Bothwell knew perfectly well what he was about when he chose the "more noisy" mode of death. Already in possession of the *Chatoullen* letters, he then had the means of compelling the Queen to marry him. Exactly this noise-making, and otherwise entirely senseless mode of murder, is a proof, little considered, but very weighty for the genuineness of the letters. From the openness of the crime these letters first obtained their peculiar value. Hence sprang, after the marriage, the curious, heretofore incomprehensible, sadness and despair of the Queen, for whom there was no alternative from submitting to the will of Bothwell, although she foresaw the consequences and was badly treated by her lover.

It is, moreover, frequently maintained, of late, that the style of the letters is too inelegant and unpolished for the Queen to have written them, and that the Sonnets are too poor to pass for the work of so good a poetess; that Mary's letters are refined, elegant, harmonious: these the opposite, "coarse, awkward and the merest patchwork," as

---

executer of the said horrible murther, as well before the committing thereof as thereafter. "Anent the retention of our Sovreane Lords Motheris Person Act, 1567, c. 19, Act Parl. III., 27." Burton, IV., p. 438. Scribner & Welford's edit., IV., 264–'5 (3).

Skelton calls them [passion, mixed with conscious guilt, does not produce fine composition].

The Sonnets, however, are by no means so bad, particularly when one compares them with those poems of the Queen on her first husband; in addition the form and [sound of the words?] as they now appear (are) probably not the original ones. Finally we possess very few really intimate and confidential letters written by the Queen.

But these (last named) letters, as, for instance, the one to the Duke of Norfolk, whom Mary had never seen, betray in their style a remarkable similarity to the style of the *Chatoullen* letters, as Burton has elegantly and strikingly shown (Labanoff, III., p. 4, 11, 18); and this fact is in a much higher degree true of the well known letter which Mary Stuart wrote under passionate excitement to Elizabeth, in which she repels the calumnies of the Countess of Shrewsbury.

Furthermore, a forger would certainly not have introduced this degree of passionateness into the letters, it lay in the character of the Queen; also, he would never have put in the numberless trifles, from doing which, it is the custom for any one to be on their guard in a forgery. Petit maintains, since other grounds of proof fail him, that the Sonnette, in which the words, "I put my son in thy hands" occur, is alone a sufficient proof of spuriousness, because the young Prince had never been in Bothwell's hands. Yet it does not read, "I have put," and it is only intended to imply that Mary with her marriage expected to leave the safety of herself and of her son trustfully in the hands of Bothwell.

Very remarkable, also, is the view of the same author, to the effect that Bothwell would, had he been in possession of the letters, infallibly have shown them to the Lords at the Ainslie Tavern, and not less remarkable, finally, that Bothwell would have destroyed the letters after the marriage, since it was for his interest to annihilate the written proofs of his guilt. They were articles of proof for Mary's guilt; for that of Bothwell there were certainly other and far more weighty ones.

It must be explained, also, that the report of de Silvas to Philip II., of 21st July, 1567, has, as Petit reviews it, been torn out of its proper connection. Elizabeth was, in the highest degree, enraged at Lethington, and the other Lords. In respect to the letters she had not yet a satisfactory understanding. Thus she could speak to de Silvas in no other way.

It is remarkable that Skelton does not completely reject the genuineness of the *Chatoullen* letters, and this shows that he had not been able to get rid of the impression of their testing by the English Commissioners, in Westminster. He thinks that they, in part, really are from the hand of the Queen, but he excepts the two dated from Glasgow and Sterling. The others, he thinks, are from Mary's hand, yet written to Darnley, and taken by the opponents of the Queen, i. e., in this case the falsifiers, from her papers, "in order to intermingle truth and falsehood, and give to the falsified parts the appearance of genuineness." He directly accuses Lethington as the falsifier, he expressly exempts Murray, for the letters were tampered with during his absence from Scotland. The accusing of Lethington is the more senseless since he (Lethington), from direct political reasons, had made the greatest efforts to prevent Murray's accusation and the production of the letters.

The conversation which Murray had with the Spanish Ambassador, de Silva, in London, on his return journey from France, is brought up by Hosack as a vindication. From what was said, however, it can only be concluded that Murray, then, had no precise knowledge in regard to the *Chatoullen* letters. But Hosack immediately concludes that another letter had been first falsified, and at a later time changed.

On the other hand, as regards direct participation in and privity to the murder of her husband by Mary Stuart, people have, up to the present time, gone somewhat too far. That Mignet should, at once, give full faith to the declarations of Bothwell's servants, which they made before their executions, has always been wonderful to me. The probability is very apparent that the accessory's accessories strove to cover themselves under the Queen's participation and approval of it.

It is, too, a decisive weight in the scale, that the chief actor, Hubert, called French Paris, did not make the compromising statements against the Queen until the second day of the examination; on the first day he, on the contrary, only described Bothwell's arrangements and activity. The conclusion is almost self-evident that his last declarations were pressed from him by the opponents of the Queen through hints of escape. Among these, especially belong the story of the costly coverlet, which the Queen caused to be brought away, shortly before the explosion. As to the (particulars) of Hubert's examination and the review of it, we know nothing. Haste was made to have him executed when he was, in the middle of June, 1569, brought to Scotland from Copenhagen by Captain Clark. As being in accordance with these points, the pretended Will of Bothwell is also brought forward by these recent authors. It has very recently been proved, in the most convincing manner, to be a forgery, although not unskilfully done, after very careful examination by Fred. Schiern, in Copenhagen.

As a new and important proof of the innocence of Mary Stuart, Hosack finally also cites an unquestionably very interesting letter from the Earl of Sussex to Cecil. This letter, however, on closer examination, contains entirely different things from what Hosack would make us believe. Sussex only says, in this letter: " It will be difficult to find ground for an accusation against the Queen, for if her opponents brought forward the letters, she might simply deny these, and justly accuse many among them of having themselves wished for the murder. So there might be better proofs." Thus, now, to draw the conclusion that Sussex considered the letters as falsified is an unhistorical and illogical proceeding, especially as Sussex, at that time, had in no way seen them. This letter is dated 22d October, 1568. That remarkable account of a contemporary (Dr. Thomas Wilson), concerning a confidential conversation, which he says he had with the Bishop of Ross, in relation to the imprisoned Queen, is also worthy of little credit as to its contents, and of doubtful meaning. The Bishop, and thus the representative of Mary Stuart, according to this conversation, not only allows the guilt of his mistress, but accuses her, most unambiguously, of killing, by poison, her first husband, the Dauphin. If Lesly really made this declaration, he appears as one of the most contemptible characters of that time, and Wilson's exclamation, " Lord, what a people, what an ambassador!" seems to be justifiable. We know too little of the personality of Wilson, and of the relations of the two men to each other, to be able to pass a clear judgment in the case. * * *

I come, finally, to the declaration of Crawford. Burton, very properly, emphasizes the weight which his testimony possesses, under any circumstances. It possessed more clearness than any statement of facts which the Lords handed in. Crawford was known as a quiet honorable man, an excellent soldier, who, at a later period, performed distinguished service. Crawford, on his oath, declared what was read to him was true and accurate, " although it was, perhaps, not in the very words." He declared that Lenox, disquieted in regard to the unexpected visit of the Queen, had begged him to take notice of all that passed. And that the King, immediately afterwards, had communicated to him the particulars of the conversation, in order that he might inform his father of them. The commissioners of Mary declined, at Westminster, to hear Crawford orally on the subject. Hosack considers it entirely impossible that any interview could be rehearsed by two eye-witnesses with such similar expressions, and instances two reports of a modern legal speech. The question, however, is here, over some few very definite questions and answers; and, besides, as already mentioned, it is not impossible that Crawford had obtained a look at the Queen's letters before he prepared his testimony. Those letters of Lenox and Wood, which asked from Crawford details in regard to the sojourn of the Queen in Glasgow, in regard to her arrival, suite, conversation, whether she sent off letters and parcels, and had received returns, only show that Lenox was gathering all the materials he could, as, indeed, Murray in like manner, without doubt, caused his *Book of Articles* to be carefully prepared.

Ziip Trest.

Mary Stuart, Queen of Scots.
From the famous portrait in the gallery of the Hermitage Palace, St. Petersburgh, Russia.
Originally in Paris, France, prior to the great French Revolution.

Bothwell's Book Mark.

CPSIA information can be obtained
at www.ICGtesting.com
Printed in the USA
LVHW080942280921
698911LV00003B/34